Anthony Jennings Bledsoe

History of Del Norte County, California

With a Business Directory and Travelers Guide

Anthony Jennings Bledsoe

History of Del Norte County, California
With a Business Directory and Travelers Guide

ISBN/EAN: 9783337210540

Printed in Europe, USA, Canada, Australia, Japan

Cover: Foto ©ninafisch / pixelio.de

More available books at **www.hansebooks.com**

HISTORY

OF

DEL NORTE COUNTY,

CALIFORNIA,

WITH A

BUSINESS DIRECTORY

AND

TRAVELER'S GUIDE.

BY A. J. BLEDSOE.

EUREKA:
HUMBOLDT TIMES PRINT—WYMAN & CO., PUBLISHERS.
1881.

To the Pioneers of California, those hardy adventurers, who bravely met untold hardships, cruel privations, and sometimes even death itself, that a new Empire might be founded on the Pacific Coast, this book is respectfully dedicated, by
                              THE AUTHOR.

PREFACE.

It was with many misgivings and doubts of success that I commenced the preparation of this book. "What! A history of Del Norte!" exclaimed the large family of the "oldest inhabitant," "why, what is there in Del Norte to write about?" Of course, these people were always ready to tell everybody by word of mouth all about the past history of Del Norte, so that it was folly to write it up. And as for the resources, industries, climate and scenery of the county, they passed by unnoticed. Whether these truthful story-tellers were color-blind, or whether, like the man who was viewing a beautiful landscape, and upon being asked what he saw, answered: "What do I see? Why, trees!" Whether, like him, the "oldest inhabitants" saw "trees," and nothing else, I know not; but certainly the "oldest inhabitants" saw nothing of the above, and it was a difficult task to gather reliable data for this work.

In my search for information I found the Know-Nothings in a very small minority, while the Know-Everythings were in such a large majority that it was almost impossible to arrive at the facts in some instances.

However, no pains have been spared to procure the best and most reliable information possible, and I cheerfully acknowledge my obligations to Benj. West, Peter Peveler, Peter Darby, Asa Thompson, W. H. Woodbury, J. K.

PREFACE.

Johnson, M. G. Tucker, J. L. Lake, F. Knox, D. Haight and W. A. Hamilton.

If this book shall be the means of awakening the citizens of Del Norte to a knowledge of the inexhaustible wealth which surrounds them on every side, waiting for the mighty arm of capital to bring it to light; if it shall direct the attention of capitalists in a single instance to the advantages offered for investment in Del Norte, then I will feel that my task has not been in vain, and that I have received an adequate compensation.

THE AUTHOR.

CRESCENT CITY, Jan. 1st, 1881.

HISTORY

OF

Del Norte County,

CALIFORNIA.

CHAPTER I.

DEL NORTE--ITS SETTLEMENT BY THE WHITES--EARLY SCENES
AND EARLY PIONEERS--HAPPY CAMP--CRESCENT
CITY--SMITH'S RIVER VALLEY--FROM
THE YEAR 1851 TO 1855.

Del Norte, signifying "the north," is situated in the north-west corner of California, and is bounded on the east by Siskiyou county, on the west by the Pacific, on the north by Curry and Josephine counties, Oregon, and on the south by Humboldt and Siskiyou counties, California; and although far removed from our metropolis, and lying in a remote part of the State, not easily accessible from the outside world, yet it was one of the first counties in the State to be settled by the whites.

In the spring of 1851 a party, consisting of Capt. S. R. Tompkins, Robt. L. Williams, Capt. McDermott, Charles Moore, Thos. J. Roach, Charles Wilson, Charles Southard, the Swain brothers, ——— Taggart, Geo. Wood, W. T. Stevens, Wm. Rumley, W. A. J. Moore, Jerry Lane, John Cox, S S. Whipple, J. W. Burke, James Buck, and several others started from Trinidad, worked their way up the

Klamath river, camping on every bar which showed the color of the gold they were seeking, and continually compelled to keep guard against the prowling and treacherous Indians. Nor was the settlement of the county effected without loss of life. For while the party were camped, some on Wingate's Bar and some on Wood's Bar, (the two bars near each other,) about eight miles below the now town of Happy Camp, three young men, named respectively Barney Ray, Moore, and Penny, concluded to go up the river on a prospecting tour. They went, and were foully murdered by the Indians, who had all along made many professions of friendship, and had in fact endeavored to induce the party to move farther up the river, saying that at a distance of less than "one half a sleep" there were good camping grounds and gold diggings.

Immediately after the massacre, which occurred a few days after the young men had arrived at their new location, several men from Wood's Bar traveled up the river to a point directly opposite the place where the young men had pitched their tent. They could see the tent still standing, but being unable to see or hear anything of the occupants, and seeing numbers of Indians skulking about the premises, they surmised that some misfortune had befallen their comrades. Actuated by this belief, they returned to camp and organized a party of volunteers to ascertain the fate of their friends. Arriving at the scene of the massacre, they found that their fears were but too well founded. The body of one of the young men, Barney Ray, was buried on the spot, and another, Penney, mortally wounded, was conveyed down the river on a litter to Wingate's Bar, where he died a short time after. The body of the other, Moore, could not be found at the time, but several weeks afterwards the remains of a dead body, supposed to have been his, was found in the river below, so much decayed as not to be recognizable. But the per petrators of the deed did not go unpunished. A portion of the party, eager to avenge the death of their comrades, pursued the Indians, and following their trail, which led up the river, discovered the Indian village, consisting of a large number of huts, and indicating the home of a large band of savages. Satisfied with their discovery, they returned to camp, and the next morning at break of day made an attack on the Indians. It is needless to say that bows and arrows were no match for the guns of the whites, and that the savages, without exception, were given a free passage and quick dispatch to the Happy Hunting Grounds. It is believed that every one of the murderers met the fate they deserved, and that not one of them escaped.

Some two or three weeks after this tragedy the party of pioneers removed from Wingate's Bar to the place afterwards called Happy Camp. And thus, ushered in by a bloody tragedy, the first settlement in Klamath (now Del Norte) county was made. For although the county had been visited by prospectors and adventurers previous to that time, it is undisputed that the Happy Camp settlement was made over a year before Crescent City was located.

Happy Camp! A name suggestive of cool shades of forest trees, sparkling streams from mountain sides; it brings with it a breath of the free, bracing air from mountain snows which fanned the cheeks of the hardy pioneers who dared to molest the Indian in his choicest hunting grounds; it suggests a land teeming with game and fruit, and all other goodly things bestowed by nature---a land in which the foot-sore and weary Argonaut might find rest at last, and end his days in peace and happiness.

But however pleasant and suggestive of peace the name may be, it is certain that the pioneers of Happy Camp met with as many difficulties as others of their class. Forced to keep a wary eye upon the Indians, compelled to prepare for the severe winter in store for them, theirs was no easy lot; nevertheless, they were one and all imbued with the energy and perseverance so characteristic of the early pioneers of California, and they were all disposed to make light of their hardships. Indeed, the place owes its name to the fact of a little celebration by the "boys" in honor of the place in which they had established their future homes. It appears that on a certain evening the whole party were assembled together and having a "high old time." The black bottle from which they refreshed the inner man was passing freely from hand to hand. And through the exhilerating effects of its contents the company were beginning to feel in accord with the spirit of the occasion, and disposed to cast dull care away and enjoy themselves while yet they might. Presently someone proposed that the place should have a name, when one of them, who perhaps was particularly satisfied with their location, suggested that it be named "Happy Camp." Immediately three hearty cheers were given for Happy Camp, the bottle was passed again, and thus the new mining town received its christening.

A short time after the settlement of Happy Camp, a settlement was made at the mouth of the Klamath river, a stream emptying into the ocean some twenty miles south of Crescent City. The Klamath was visited in 1850 by a schooner on a voyage of exploration, which anchored off the mouth of the river and sent a small boat with a crew of fifteen or twenty to make an attempt to cross the bar. The bar being rough at the time, the boat was swamped, and all the crew were drowned with the exception of one man, who was rescued by the Indians. Afterwards, in the year 1851, another schooner arrived and a settlement was formed. It was supposed that the Klamath river was rich in gold, and the new town soon became the headquarters of explorers, prospectors, and others. It was named Klamath City, and it had a rapid growth.

The frames of houses, ready to be put together on arrival, were shipped by sail vessels from San Francisco, and it is said that one iron house was imported and erected in the town. For what purpose it was intended or used is not known. As the Indians were living there in great numbers, it is supposed that the owner intended to guard against their attacks by erecting a castle which would be proof against shot and fire.

As before stated, Klamath City had a rapid growth, and soon became a place of considerable importance. But its growth was not more rapid than its decline, and it had but a brief existence. Prospectors at the mouth of the river did not meet with the success they had anticipated, and they soon began to seek other mining localities. Expeditions were fitted out to explore the upper Klamath, which, with the exception of that part near its mouth, was as great a mystery as the headwaters of the Nile. In 1852 the iron house was re-shipped to San Francisco, and a short time afterwards Klamath City belonged to the list of deserted mining towns.

The California Legislature of 1851-2 provided for the organization of Klamath county, and ordered an election to be held on the second Monday in June, 1851. The Act was approved on May 28, 1851, and R. A. Parker, W. W. Hawks, Edward Fletcher, Smith Clark and B. W. Dullitt, of said county, were appointed and constituted a Board of Commissioners to designate the election precincts for such election. The officers were duly elected and the county government took effect immediately after.

Crescent City was the next place in the county to be settled by the whites, and it seems somewhat strange that it should not have been permanently settled before the year 1852. As early as the spring of 1850 a schooner, the Paragon, arrived in the harbor, and was wrecked on the beach below the site of the present town; and in the same year, and also in 1851, parties of prospectors visited the place, but for some reason made no settlement there.

And like many other towns in California, Crescent City owes its origin to that insatiable thirst for gold which actuated and controlled the movements of all the early immigrants to the shores of the Pacific.

In 1849--50 a story was circulated throughout the Pacific Coast and in many parts of the East, rivaling the legend of Captain Kidd's hidden treasure, and surpassing in imaginative qualities any fable of the "Arabian Nights." There are many versions of the story, but the one the writer remembers to have heard is as follows:

In the early days of the mining excitement in California, a miner, more adventurous than any of his fellows, armed with his trusty rifle and supplied with necessary mining implements, crossed the rugged Coast Range and prospected the gulches and ravines of the foot-hills near the sea shore. One lucky day he "struck it rich." The rich earth yielded its yellow treasures in abundance, and the solitary miner, with no one at first to molest him, erected a cabin in the wilderness, with the sole thought of amassing a fortune and returning to home and friends in San Francisco.

And there, in the midst of the "forest primeval," with the giant trees, "standing like Druids of old," towering above him, the lonely gold-hunter toiled as if for life; and day after day, for many weary months, added to his store of wealth, until the time drew near when he could return to his home with his pockets heavy with hard-earned gold-dust But the prowling Indian, ever eager for the blood of the white man, found his retreat at last, and attacking him with overwhelming numbers, left him senseless on the ground, apparently dead. The miner's treasure was too well hidden to be easily found, and failing in their search for it, the savages set fire to the cabin, burning it to the ground. After they had left the miner recovered consciousness, but not his reason—the light of his mind had gone out, and left a flickering flame of disconnected thoughts. Bereft of his reason, he wandered out of the forest and into the home of civilization. How he succeeded in finding his way back to his friends in San Francisco the legend saith not. But (so the story goes) he did succeed in making his way back to his home, and there, after a short time, died. Before his death his reason returned to him, and calling his friends around him, he told them the story of his hidden treasure, describing minutely the locality of the cabin, and from the account he gave it was evident that the lost cabin was situated somewhere on the northern coast of California.

So runs the legend of the lost cabin. And however improbable the story may appear, it is certain that it was, in various forms, circulated far and wide, and that many parties were at different times fitted out to search for the bonanza. In the spring of 1851 a party under Capt. McDermott were searching for the lost cabin in the vicinity of what is now known as French Hill. Ascending to the top of the hill, they saw before them a broad expanse of ocean, with here and there an indentation in the coast line, and at one spot in particular a deep indentation in the rocky coast caused them to believe that there was to be found a bay of considerable extent.

Fully convinced of this fact, the party were not long in circulating the report, and in September, 1852, another party, consisting of Capt. Bell, Major J. B. Taylor, Henry Kennedy, Thomas McGrew, James D. Mace, Richard Humphreys, Wm. Osborn, and a few others started for the coast in search of the now Crescent City harbor. They procured the necessary outfit at Althouse creek, Oregon, and were well prepared for the then perilous and fatigueing journey. They were obliged to cut trails for themselves and animals, and met with numerous obstacles which required great perseverance and labor to surmount.

At last reaching the coast, they passed through a valley near the foot-hills, and were surprised to find large herds of elk feeding quietly by the way, seemingly unmindful of their presence. For this reason the valley was named Elk valley, which name it bears at the present time.

Arriving at the seashore, the party camped near the beach, and as winter was approaching, their first thought was to prepare for it. And as their provisions were becoming exhausted, they dispatched a messenger, Richard Humphreys, to San Francisco, instructing him to charter a schooner from that port to Paragon (now Crescent City) Bay.

While in San Francisco, Richard Humphreys met J. F. Wendell, and induced him to organize an expedition to Point St. George. The expedition was soon organized and equipped, and chartering the schooner Pomona, they set sail and arrived at Paragon Bay sometime during the fall of 1852.

Nothing was done, however, during the year 1852 toward laying out the town of Crescent City, and it was not until the month of February, 1853, that any move was made in that direction. During the winter of 1852-3 A. M. Rosborough purchased a land warrant in J. F. Wendell's name for the 320 acres of land on which Crescent City now stands, and in February, 1853, the land was surveyed by T. P. Robinson and divided up into town lots. It has always been supposed that all of the locators of Crescent City were equally interested in the purchase and distribution of these lots; but from the records on file in the County Clerk's office, it would appear that such was not the case. Lots in the new town were transferred by deed from J. F. Wendell to the following named persons: W. A. Thorp, A. M. Rosborough, G. W. Jordan. A. K. Ward, R. Humphreys, J. M Peters, J. K. Irving, J. D. Cook, J. B. Taylor, B. J. Bell, W. S. Watterman, F. E. Weston, P. C. Bryant, M. Martin, M. Smythe, A. Coyle,

C. D. Poston, G. A. Guthrie, H. Fellows, T. H. McGrew, D. C. Lewis, H. Kennedy, J. M. Pugh, J. H. Short, T. S. Pomeroy, J. H. Boddeby, S. T. Watts and H. S. Fitch; and it appears from the deeds that all the above named, except seven, received their lots for a money consideration, ranging from $100 to $1,000, and that but six of the party besides J. F. Wendell were originally interested in any portion of said land. The transfer to W. A. Thorp was in consideration of having "rendered services in and about Point St. George," and the following named received their deeds in consideration of having "contributed equally with J. F. Wendell of their money, labor and materials in fitting out an expedition to Point St. George:" F. E. Weston, G. W. Jordan, A. K. Ward, R. Humphreys, J. M. Peters and J. K. Irving. Therefore, as only Weston, Jordan, Ward, Humphreys, Peters, Irving and Wendell had invested their means in the enterprise, these gentlemen should be looked upon as the founders of Crescent City.

The grant which Wendell had purchased from the State was, however, afterwards declared to be void, the United States Government claiming the right to the land, and those who had invested in town lots were in danger of losing both their lots and money. An arrangement was finally effected by which the Common Council of Crescent City purchased the land from the United States, at $2 50 per acre. The Council then issued certificates of title to all those who had bought town lots from Wendell, and to those who were originally interested in the location of the town. When the town was located it was named Crescent City, because the bay on which it is situated is in the form of a semi-circle.

In 1853 many people were constantly arriving at Crescent City, and the place was rapidly growing from a small collection of tents to a good-sized town. Among the first arrivals were James Brooking, Alexander Coyle,

Samuel Watts, M. V. Jones, John White, Peter Peveler, Daniel Haight, James Haight, Oliver Charter, Benj. West, E. G. Hayes, Ray Wallace, J. K. Johnson, John Malone, J. G. Wall, Peter Darby, Sam. Crandall, Asa Thompson, Major Bradford, H. Davis, E. L. Magruder, W. H. Hamilton, and others.

The first vessel to arrive after the wreck of the Paragon in 1850 was the schooner Pomona, which arrived sometime in the fall of '52. The next vessel to arrive was the San Francisco, Capt. Goodwin, which anchored in Crescent City harbor on the 6th of May, 1853. having on board as passengers Messrs. Gilbert, Steel, Hoover, Crandall, Terry, Farrington, Deitrich, Dickson, West, Myers, and a man called "Dock." Gilbert & Farrington, who established the first store here, had on board 40 or 50 tons of assorted merchandise.

The first mercantile firms who opened business at Crescent City were S. H. Grubler, Gilbert & Farrington, Hamilton & Co., and a short time afterward Gilkey & Co., G. W. Jordan, John Y. Valentine, Crowell & Fairfield, J. B. Rosborough, Messer & Co., J. W. Stateler and J. J. Friedman & Co. W. A. Hamilton, who established the third mercantile house here, arrived on the schooner Pomona, in the month of May, a short time after the arrival of the San Francisco, having with him a large stock of general merchandise. On board the schooner was a lighter, capable of carrying 4 or 5 tons, which had been brought from San Francisco for the express purpose of landing the schooner's cargo. The goods were loaded on the lighter, and it being run as far up on the beach as possible, they were packed through the surf to the shore. The supplies at Althouse and other places had almost given out, and a large crowd had assembled on the beach ready to buy the goods as they were landed from the lighter. Before sunset on the same day they were landed from the schooner, $1,500 worth of goods were sold without removing them from the beach. This was doing a rushing business on very short notice.

F. E. Weston, who it has been said was one of the party to found Crescent City, had no individual interest in the expedition, but represented R. F. Knox & Co., of San Francisco, who sent Weston to represent and take charge of their interests. They bought and shipped in his charge on the Pomona a small saw-mill, which he immediately erected near what is now the corner of C and Third streets. That mill made the lumber of which the first houses in Crescent City were constructed. A year or two later they built a larger saw-mill near the corner of G and Seventh streets, and in 1856 they added a grist mill. The first sack of flour ever ground in this county was turned out of the Crescent City Mills in October, 1856. In 1857 Mr. Weston left and S. G. Kingsland took his place in charge of the property and business. In 1860 these mills were burned down, with all the surrounding improvements with the exception of the house now occupied by Judge Hamilton, and a large amount of lumber and grain was consumed at the same time.

Among the arrivals at Crescent City during the month of April, 1853, were James Haight, D. Haight, H. Davis, ——— Dominee, and one or two others who in the month of August of the same year made the first settlement in Smith's River Valley, locating on the north side of Rowdy Creek. They found the country covered with high fern or brake, ten feet high in places. Plenty of game could be found throughout the valley, there being large numbers of elk, deer, bear, wild geese, ducks, pheasants, etc. The elk, especially, were to be found in large numbers, and for a long time furnished the settlers with the most delicious meat.

The south side of Rowdy Creek was soon after settled by H. W. Jones, the Wallace brothers, John Leverton, and others, and both sides were constantly receiving accessions to their population.

Running through the valley is Smith's River, from which the valley received its name. Much speculation has been given to the subject of how the river first received its name, and no definite conclusion has ever been arrived at as to how or when it was named. It is certain that as far back as the earliest settlement of the northern country it was known by its present name.

The most generally accepted account of its origin is, that sometime in 1838 or 1839 a company of men in the employ of the Hudson Bay Company traveled down the coast from the Columbia river, and camping on the banks of the river which now bears the Captain's name, were murdered by the Indians. At the present time there are no records, or persons living to substantiate the above account, and besides it is evident that it has no foundation in truth. The river undoubtedly owes its name to the ignorance of the early explorers and traders in regard to the topography of the northern coast.

In 1842 Fremont camped on the shore of Klamath Lake, Oregon, and in his account of his second voyage of exploration he remarks that he was forced to take extra precautions to guard against the Indians, and says, "I was not unmindful of the fate of Captain Smith and party." From this it would seem certain that a man named Smith was murdered by the Indians, and it is equally certain that his name was given to another river, which empties into Rogue river, in Oregon.

In the time of Fremont's voyage, and long after, a river in Oregon, now known as Illinois river, was called Smith's river; and it was supposed to empty into the ocean somewhere near the mouth of the present Smith's river. It was natural, therefore, that those who crossed the mountains and traveled down this river to the coast should call the stream Smith's river, believing, as they did, that the two rivers were one and the same. In the course of time, when the country became better known, the true Smith's river received the new name of Illinois, while the Del Norte river retained the former name and has kept it ever since.

The first white child ever born in Del Norte county was born in Crescent City to the wife of Mr. Frame, on the 28th day of August, 1853, and was christened "Mary Frame"

The town of Crescent City was rapidly improving, the population of the county was steadily increasing, and business houses and dwellings were being erected on every hand.

And about this time the influence of the white settlement was being felt by the Indians; they were being pushed to the wall by the march of civilization. In the spring of 1853 a man called California Jack, accompanied by several others, started from Crescent City on a prospecting tour, intending to visit some place near Smith's river. A short time afterwards an Indian was seen in town carrying a revolver with the name, "California Jack," engraved upon it. Surmising that the prospectors had been murdered by the Indians, a party of citizens attacked the Indians on Battery Point, near town, killing the one who had the pistol and several others. A company was immediately organized to search for the supposed murdered men. The camp of the prospectors on the banks of Smith's river was easily found, and further search resulted in the discovery of the bodies of the men, all bearing marks of violence by the Indians.

After the punishment of the Indians at Battery Point, a large number of the survivors removed to a rancheria near the mouth of Smith's river, known as the Yontocket ranch. But the feeling in Crescent City against them was too intense to subside without a further punishment being administered. A company was formed, and procuring a guide who had some knowledge of the country, they with difficulty made their way through the forests, and arriving at a point near the ranch, prepared for the attack on the Indians. Of the manner in which the attack was made, no authentic information can now be obtained. It is well known, however, that the fight ended in a disastrous defeat to the savages, a large number being killed, while the whites escaped with little or no loss.

Other murders were committed in the same year by the Indians, the accounts of which are meager and not thoroughly reliable. One account says that in the neighborhood of what is now known as Shannon's creek, a few miles north of Smith's river, three men who were traveling down the coast were attacked and murdered by the Indians, their bodies being hidden in a cave in the rocks, and afterwards found. Other difficulties between the whites and Indians occurred at intervals, the adventurous spirit of the whites and the reluctance of the Indians to give up their lands to them, causing the breach to grow wider and wider, until it threatened to involve the county in a general Indian war.

The summer of 1853 passed quietly away, with but little excitement, except an occasional murder by the Indians, and the patriotic celebration of the Fourth of July, the first celebration of the day we honor ever held in Crescent City. During the fall the steamer Columbia made regular trips from San Francisco to Crescent City, heavily laden with freight and passengers. A number of sailing vessels were also making regular trips, carrying freight and passengers.

It was during the spring and summer of '54 that the most remarkable improvements were made in Crescent City. Money was plentiful, wages were high and laborers in demand, the mines were beginning to attract attention, and everything indicated that a lively city would be built up in this remote corner of California.

The year 1854, especially, opened most auspiciously for Crescent City. Nor was the rest of the county behind. The whole county was becoming settled with people from all parts of the Union, and from nearly every part of the civilized world.

On the 10th of June that necessity of all civilized communities, a local newspaper, was established, with Messrs. B. F. Fechtig and W. B. Freaner as publishers. It was called the Crescent City Herald, was a five-column paper, published all at home, and ably edited.

The mail service at that time lacked much of being what it is to-day. An accommodation mail was carried by the steamers, and during the summer was received regularly once in two weeks. When winter came, however, it was a fortunate circumstance if a mail was received once a month. Crescent City had perhaps better mail facilities than other parts of the county; and Smith's River Valley, especially, was fortunate indeed if it received a mail once a month.

As before remarked, the town and county were rapidly improving. Large numbers of people were attracted hither by the mineral and agricultural resources which were known to exist in the immediate vicinity of Crescent City. The mining region lying back of the town was thought to be among the best and richest in the State. And although the expectations of the miners in regard to the lasting qualities of the placer mines were not fully realized, yet the mines "panned out" exceedingly well, and the deposits were sufficiently abundant to cause a considerable excitement in regard to them. The miners on Myrtle creek, twelve miles from town, were doing exceedingly well. The general average was from five to fifteen dollars per day to the hand, and in the month of June one man took out, in two hours, four hundred dollars. New diggings were discovered on the South Fork of Smith's river, and in other parts of the county. The miners on Smith's river were making from ten to twenty-five dollars per day to the hand, while laborers were making from one hundred to one hundred and fifty dollars per month. New diggings were discovered on Indian creek, near Happy Camp, which proved to be very rich. They prospected from $1 to $3 to the pan. Laborers on Indian creek were getting $100 per month and found. On the Klamath river miners were meeting with extraordinary success. New and rich diggings were daily being discovered, and the mines yielded from $20 to $40 per day to the hand. At Happy Camp, several large ditches were constructed, thus commencing the extensive system of ditches and flumes that now furnish water to nearly all the bars in the vicinity Gold was also discovered on the middle fork of Indian creek, a tributary of the Klamath, and a lively mining camp was soon established there. Some twenty houses were erected and about eighty miners were at work, making from $9 to $15 per day to the hand.

Twelve miles from the above named diggings, situated on the Klamath at the mouth of Indian creek, were the Happy Camp diggings. At that time the village of Happy Camp consisted of six or eight houses, the placers lying scattered in the neighborhood. About sixty miners were working here, averaging from $5 to $12 per day to the hand. A short distance below Happy Camp, on Elk creek, a stream running from the south into the Klamath river, new diggings were struck, yielding from $10 to $15 per day to the hand. On the 4th of November new diggings were discovered on a creek running from the redwood ridge and emptying into Smith's river near the ferry then owned by White & Miller, now known as Peacock's ferry. The mines were about six miles from Crescent City. Dirt paying from three to five cents per pan was found in large quantities, and some claims were worked which panned out from ten to twenty cents to the pan.

Nor were prospectors for the golden treasure content

to confine their operations to the mountains, gulches and ravines—they even staked off the beach in front of Crescent City into mining claims. But eventually it was ascertained that the sand was not of sufficient value to repay the expense of working the same, and the claims were abandoned to the winter revels of old Neptune, who gave his first notice "to quit" by the loud blast of a "sou-easter."

And the agricultural interests of the county were not neglected. During the spring and summer of '54 nearly seventy-five farmers located in various parts of the county, and rapidly brought into cultivation much of fertile land. The first crops raised in the county were raised in Smith's River Valley by Ray Wallace and T. Crook, and were harvested in the above named year. The seed was mostly obtained from Oregon, being brought across the mountains by pack trains. Vegetables in large quantities were also raised, and daily and weekly supplies were received at Crescent City from the surrounding country. In addition to cultivating the land already cleared, the farmers were also busily engaged in clearing more land, building houses and fences, setting out fruit trees, etc.

But however rapid was the development of the mining and agricultural resources of the county, they could not keep pace with the extraordinary growth and improvement of Crescent City. In the spring of '53 there was but one house standing on the present site of Crescent City. In the spring of '54 the town contained nearly three hundred houses, with a population of between eight hundred and a thousand inhabitants. Like the mining towns in the good old days of '49 and '50, it had sprung up as if by magic, and demonstrated the fact that "a city may be born in a day."

And in accord with the marvelous growth of the town, was the extraordinary and far-reaching enterprise of its citizens. Every day some new project for the improvement of the place was set on foot and energetically carried forward to completion. Hotels and business houses were constantly being opened to the public, the town was rapidly encroaching upon the adjacent forests, and buildings were even erected on the beach; secret societies and orders were formed, and a fire department was organized; saloons and billiard halls flourished in close proximity to the only house of God the place supported; in fact, it soon became the type of a California mining town. The streets were filled with people and presented a busy scene --the miner from the mountains jostled the farmer from the valley; the merchant and the trader vied with each other in the use of the cunning arguments of trade; speculators in town lots talked loudly to new comers of the advantages of this, "the garden spot of God's green earth, God bless you, sir;" young men from the States, eager to join the great army who were searching for gold, bartered for animals and outfits; pack trains just in from across the mountains, passed other trains preparing to start on their trip across the Siskiyous, heavily laden with merchandise and mining implements.

Several express companies were doing a rushing business, including Leland & McCombe's express (connecting at San Francisco with Wells, Fargo & Co.,) and Adams & Co., who also had connections in San Francisco.

Crescent City was becoming the center of a large and increasing trade, and her merchants soon began to agitate the question of building a wagon road to Illinois valley, O. T. Good roads are a prime necessity of civilization, and realizing this fact, the people of Crescent City held a public meeting on the 10th of June, 1854, to devise means to build the road, having previously subscribed $6,000 toward the enterprise. At the meeting referred to, the preliminary organization for the formation of a Joint-Stock Company, to build a plank and turnpike road, was completed, twenty-five citizens comprising the company of preliminary organization. Hon. S. G. Whipple was elected President, F. E. Weston, Secretary, and S. H. Grubler, Treasurer. The corporate name was declared to be, "The Crescent City and Yreka Plank and Turnpike Company," and a resolution was offered and passed "That the President, Secretary and Treasurer are hereby constituted a Board of Directors for this Company;" and the Directors were empowered to employ a competent Engineer to survey the road, and also to employ suitable persons to assist in the looking-out and survey of different routes.

In the meantime, while this question was being agitated among the citizens, an "Act to Incorporate Crescent City" passed both houses of the Legislature in April, 1854, received the signature of the Governor, and became a law. This Act defined the limits of Crescent City as follows:

"The boundaries of Crescent City shall be as follows: Commencing at a point established by T. P. Robinson, County Surveyor of Klamath county, east of Elk creek, running thence south to low water mark, and north twenty-five chains and ——— links; thence west one mile; thence south to low water mark, and thence following low water mark to the intersection of the east line."

After the passage of this Act the town began to put on city airs. A full-fledged Common Council was let loose upon the public treasury, constables were elected, marshals were appointed, and a complete organization of the city government effected.

And about the same time, the question of the boundary line between California and O. T. was permanently settled. The disputed territory comprised all that mining country in and about Sailor Diggings and Althouse creek---a country abounding in precious metals, and the possession of which would have been a valuable addition to the mineral wealth of Del Norte. In June, 1854, a surveying party under T. P. Robinson surveyed the northern boundary of the State of California, and decided that the disputed territory belonged to O. T., and not California, as was generally supposed. The decision caused some excitement in the neighborhood of Sailor Diggings and Althouse creek, as the miners did not like to be so suddenly transported from California to Oregon. They had before both voted in California and O. T., and had refused to pay taxes to either.

On Thursday, June 22, 1854, occurred one of those shocking tragedies so common in the early history of California. It appears that a young man named James T. Kelley, in company with another young man named A. K. Ward, joined a party for the purpose of serenading some of the citizens of the place. At the time the fatal blow was struck Kelley was playing on the violin, and it is supposed that the bow struck Ward on the arm, when he (Ward) exclaimed, "Don't draw that on me!" and stabbed him (Kelley) in the region of the heart. A doctor was called, but his skill was of no avail. The wounded man spoke but three words--"I am killed"--and expired in a few minutes. Immediately after the commission of the murder, Ward was arrested, and after examination lodged in jail to await his trial. He afterwards broke jail, but was captured in Sacramento some months later. He was tried at Yreka in 1855 and acquitted. Although the murderer was acquitted of the charge against him, yet the affray was a striking commentary on the evil influence of intoxicating drinks, as the evidence adduced at the trial disclosed the fact that all the parties were in a state of intoxication at the time of the killing.

Saturday, June 24th, the first Masonic celebration ever held in Del Norte county was held in honor of the anniversary of St. John. The oration was delivered by Dr. E. Mason. At 2 o'clock a dinner was served at the Oriental Hotel, at which there was a convivial flow of good feeling. The regular toasts were:

"Our Master—As the sun continues to shed abroad his light by day, and the moon to illume the night, so may our Master prove the reflection of both.

Our Senior Warden—As the clear, blue sky is to the sun, and the bright twinkling stars to the moon, so may the Senior Warden ever be to the Master."

The survey of the route for the Crescent City and Yreka plank and turnpike road was completed by T. P. Robinson in October, and a subscription book was opened by the Company. The capital stock was fixed at $85,000, divided into 850 shares of $100 each, and before the end of the year subscriptions to the amount of $18,500 were received.

During the year, in the month of August, the first vessel built at Crescent City was launched, being named the Rosalie, commanded by E. A. Babcock, and built for S. T. Crowther, of San Francisco. She was a small schooner, 9 feet deep and measuring 53 tons. She was built of spruce and hemlock, and was intended for the bay trade at San Francisco.

Toward the close of the year 1854 the trade of Crescent City had grown to quite respectable proportions The steamers Major Tompkins, America, Columbia, Crescent City, and Fremont were making regular trips between San Francisco, Crescent City and the Columbia river. A number of schooners were also making regular trips. The inland transportation was confined to pack trains, of which there were large numbers engaged in carrying merchandise from wholesale houses in Crescent City to Happy Camp. Althouse. Sailor Diggings and other points in Southern Oregon.

Below will be found the trade of Crescent City for the period of seven months from March 16th to October 22, 1854. For a town at that time only nineteen months old. its harbor at times insecure, its outlets only mountain trails, it is certainly a wonderful and creditable showing, indicating on the part of its merchants a degree of business enterprise worthy to be imitated at the present time.

The number of arrivals, according to the Custom House reports, were, steamers, 39; sailing vessels, 9; total, 48. Amount of freight carried by steamers, 3,385 tons; by sailing vessels, 540; total, 3,925; or, in round numbers, 4,000 tons of merchandise.

During the same period the number of passengers carried from San Francisco to Crescent City, according to the Purser's reports, was 2,286.

Thus it will be seen that the travel to this part of the State was very large, and that its many natural advantages were at that time receiving the attention they deserved.

About the 1st of November a tragedy occurred which was the direct cause of bringing about difficulties between the whites and Indians. Mr. A. French, a farmer living about three miles from Crescent City, went on a hunt with a party of three others to the South Fork of Smith's River, camping on the Bald Hills, about ten miles from town. It was agreed that French should return home on the following Thursday, while the rest of the party were to continue their hunt a few days longer. French left the camp on Thursday morning, the rest of the party supposing that he had returned to his home. But when they arrived at Crescent City on Saturday evening they were met by Mrs. French, inquiring for her husband. He had not returned home, and nothing had been seen or heard of him.

It was at once suspicioned that the Indians on the South Fork of Smith's River had murdered the missing man. The citizens, with their usual promptness in cases of the kind, appointed a committee to apprehend all the Indians about town and in the neighborhood. But little information was gained from them; nevertheless, the suspicion that French had been murdered became more of a certainty, and parties were sent out to hunt for the body.

On Mill creek, (a tributary of Smith's River,) was a rancheria where the Indians of the coast were wont to resort for the purpose of laying in a supply of acorns for the winter. At this rancheria a party headed by J. M. Rosborough examined the Indians thoroughly, and from the knowledge derived from them it appeared that in the latter part of October an Indian from Chetcoe (24 miles up the coast, in Oregon,) had made a proposal to a Klamath Indian called Black Mow to kill a white man. Black Mow refused, saying that he lived in peace with the whites, and had been for years in the habit of ferrying them across the Klamath. The Chetcoe Indian then offered him the squaw standing by, which offer proved irresistible, and Black Mow answered "soon"

After gaining this information, Rosborough and his men had little difficulty in finding the body. They found it laying under a log and partly covered up, the wild animals of the forest having meanwhile attacked and devoured part of it. With the exception of the hat, none of the clothing was missing, and even a gold ring on his finger was there still. The remains were buried near the spot where they were found, and the party returning to Crescent City, a writ was issued for the apprehension of the Indians Black Mow, Jim and Narpa, accused of the murder of A. French. Mr. Kennedy, Lieutenant of the Company of Klamath Rangers, was deputized to pursue the guilty parties, commanding a party of seven men, namely, T. B. Thorp, Israel Deitrich, T. H. McGrew, —— Leaks, J. R. Sloan, J. H. Ritchie and J. B. Rosborough. The Indians were captured at the mouth of the Klamath, and were taken to Crescent City on the 17th of November.

On the day following the citizens of Crescent City assembled en masse at the Eldorado Saloon, on Front street, and organized by calling E. Mason, Esq., to the Chair, and appointing S. G. Whipple, Secretary. The Chairman stated the object of the meeting to be, the trial of the three Indians then in custody, (and if the evidence should warrant a conviction, the jury to award the punishment,) namely, Black Mow, his son Jim, Klamath Indians, and a Chetcoe Indian called Narpa, accused of the murder of A. French.

On motion, the following named gentlemen were appointed jurors: D. W. McComb, J. B. Taylor, J F. Wendell, T. B. Thorp, Richard Barnes. Jacob Lance, M. G. Tucker, T. S. Sanford. T. S Pomeroy, John Miller, J. R. Sloan and Benj. West.

The presiding Judge was Judge Lynch, well known in the early days of California, whose decrees were always final, from which no appeal could be taken. And however unjust and cruel their mode of trial may be deemed at the present time, the early settlers of California were justified in resorting to such extreme measures. Not only is it asserted in the law, but it is, and always has been instinctively felt that "Self-preservation is the first law of Nature." Mankind, in all ages, has recognized the necessity of disregarding the established rules of the law, whenever that law, through its own inherent defects, or because of its non-enforcement by the proper officers, has failed to afford the protection to life and property for which it was intended.

In the early days of Del Norte, the Judicial system then in force allowed of but few sittings of the courts of justice in this county; therefore, prisoners lodged in jail awaiting trial were liable to make their escape. The jail at Crescent City was a wooden building, affording but slight security against the escape of its inmates. And it is not surprising that the citizens, rather than run the risk of losing the chance to punish the murderers as they deserved, should take the law into their own hands.

The jury in the trial of the murderers of French, after an absence of one hour, returned a verdict of "guilty," and sentenced the murderers to be hanged on Monday, Nov. 24th, 1854, at 12 o'clock, M.

On motion, J. R. Sloan, Richard Barnes and Capt. John Boddeby were appointed a committee to execute the sentence of the jury.

At the appointed time Black Mow, Jim and Narpa were taken from the jail and hung near Battery Point, a large number of spectators being present. The ropes were tied to the limb of a tree, and the other ends being fastened around the necks of the culprits, the wagon upon which they were standing was driven from under them, and in a few seconds the case was transferred to a Higher Tribunal, and the souls of three guilty Indians sent to account before the Great Spirit who watches over all.

Before the close of the year the consequences of the French tragedy began to be experienced. At a meeting of the citizens of Smith's River Valley, held at the house of Major Bradford, to devise some means for finding out the nature of some alleged threats made by the Indians in the vicinity, a committee was appointed to make investigations, consisting of Dr. Myers, John Leverton, John Vaughan and W. Carman. The committee visited the Indian rancheria in the vicinity, and from their report it appears that the circumstances causing a suspicion of a plot against the whites were as follows: The presence of Rogue River, Chetcoe and Klamath Indians---the removal of their provisions---the discovery of secret and carefully concealed paths by which the different tribes communicated with each other. These facts were sufficient to arouse the fears of the people of the valley, and a careful watch was kept of the movements of the Indians.

CHAPTER II.

COUNTY GOVERNMENT MATTERS---THE STATE CAPITAL---THE KLAMATH RESERVATION-- BURNING OF THE AMERICA---THE COUNTY OF DEL NORTE CREATED--INDIAN TROUBLES-- FROM 1854 TO 1860.

About the 1st of January, 1855, the difficulties between the whites and Indians terminated in a fight on the Lake, four miles from Crescent City, in which about thirty Indians were killed. The two Companies, the Coast and Klamath Rangers, took jointly part in the affair, assisted by the settlers in Smith's River Valley. A treaty of peace was afterwards made with the Smith's River Indians by the people of the valley. In February an Indian war broke out on the upper Klamath, in which several whites were killed, ferry boats cut away, etc. A detachment of soldiers were sent from Humboldt Bay to the scene of the trouble, and by their aid the savages were quelled.

On the 22d of February, 1855, the first celebration of Washington's birthay in Crescent City took place. There was a parade during the day, but the ball in the evening at the No. 8 Hotel was the great attraction on this occasion.

The express company of Wells, Fargo & Co. established a branch office in Crescent City, appointing as agent D. W. McCombe. About the same time news was received by steamer that the banking houses and express companies of both Adams & Co., and Wells, Fargo & Co., had went down in the great storm of business failures which swept over the country in 1855. The news caused no unusual run on the branch office of Wells, Fargo & Co. at Crescent City, but the house of Adams & Co. was besieged by excited depositors, eagerly claiming their money. In one day, between 4 and 10 A. M., the sum of $11,809.16 was paid out by E. G. Wescott, the agent here. All the demands against the Crescent City branch of Adams & Co. were paid, with the exception of $626 due to four individuals whose whereabouts were unknown.

It seems that Klamath county was as badly governed as any county in the State. Many and loud were the complaints in regard to the financial condition of the county, and much attention was called to the fact that Klamath county, although not quite four years old, was over $13,000 in debt, without roads, without county buildings, even without a proper safe for her records.

The Court of Sessions, a Judiciary tribunal, had been entrusted with the management of county affairs in general, in all the counties of the State, except San Francisco The Court of Sessions of Klamath county had, so far as the administration and general supervision of county affairs was concerned, made a complete failure in that particular line of business, and involved the county in debt at a time when it should have had a balance standing in its favor.

It is no wonder, then, that a change in the county government was hailed with satisfaction by the tax-payers of the county. The change consisted in an Act by the Legislature, transferring the management of county affairs to a Board of Supervisors.

The Legislature of 1854–5 had under consideration the subject of locating permanently the capital of the State, and among the places proposed and discussed as being suitable for that purpose was Crescent City.

What a wonderful Legislature that must have been! What a number of valuable town lots must have been offered its members to induce them to propose as the capital of the State, a town in the extreme north-west corner, and at that time almost inaccessible during the winter months. What an immense amount of ignorance must have been concentrated in that legislative body of the days of '55! Even in these days of Kearneyism and sand-lot legislation, it excites our admiration, in contemplating the sublime ignorance of the country displayed by this early Legislature.

Unfortunately for Crescent City, the bill removing the State capital to that place failed to pass, and the visions of town lot speculators vanished into thin air. But the Crescentonians were bouyant with life and energy, and the news of the failure was but a passing cloud across their bright hopes and expectations. No doubt, as the principal men of the place discussed the matter over their wine and cigars, new speculations and day-dreams of future greatness served to "Solace the hopes that ended in smoke!"

In April Happy Camp was thrown into a state of great excitement by a murder on Indian creek, and Judge Lynch was again called on to pass sentence on a criminal The quarrel from which the murder arose originated in the store of a Mr. Smith, about a pipe which a man by the name of McFarlan James accused one Phillips of having taken from his pocket. Angry words ensued, which led to a fight between the two, when James received a mortal wound. Phillips threw away his knife and escaped, but was overtaken between Indian Creek and Happy Camp and taken back to the former place.

A meeting of the miners was called, and Col. James Taylor made Chairman, E. H. Scovel, Secretary, Perry

Masters, Constable, and John Ware, Deputy. C. Wallace offered a resolution to take the voice of the assembled miners as to the propriety of trying J. A. Phillips by them, or handing him over to the civil authorities. It was resolved to try him by the miners. A committee was appointed to collect the evidence. C. Wallace and A. Boyce acting as counsel for the State, and S. Boyce and John S. Sands for the prisoner. The jury returned a verdict of "guilty," and the prisoner was hung at 10 o'clock, A. M., March 31st, 1855.

Arrangements for an Indian reservation on the Klamath were completed in April. 1855, by S. G. Whipple, Indian Agent for Klamath county; the reservation to extend from the mouth of the Klamath twenty miles up the river, and two miles in width. Mr. Whipple took with him to the reservation some agricultural implements, tools, seeds, a supply of twine for fishing nets, etc, for the use of the Indians. About 1500 Indians, of every age and sex, were on the reservation, living in some 150 huts. Mr. Whipple engaged the services of H. B. Dickinson, of Crescent City, to instruct the Indians in the various duties and pursuits which their location on the reservation might necessitate.

The number of Indians in Klamath county at that time was variously estimated at from 3000 to 5000, living mostly on the Klamath and its tributaries, and the necessity for a reservation had long been felt.

In June a company was formed in Crescent City for the purpose of whaling. Whales had frequently shown themselves in large numbers in and near the harbor, and it was thought that the whaling business would prove a profitable one. The company established works for trying out the oil on Whale island, a large rock, containing about ten acres, situated in the bay, and offering a convenient and safe place for the purpose.

During the summer of 1855 business continued good, and the merchants were extending their trade by every means within their power. A sum of money, amounting to $4100, was raised by subscription for the purpose of opening a trail from Crescent City to the Klamath, which would shorten the route between Crescent City and Yreka. The trail was completed by the contractors in August, of the same year.

Sunday, June 24th, 1855, was a memorable day for Crescent City, and the event which made it so will long be remembered by the early settlers of the county. At 3:20 o'clock on the afternoon of that day, the side-wheel steamship America, A. G. Jones, Commanding, anchored in the harbor, en route for Puget Sound, to which point she was bound with the 21st U. S. Infantry, numbering 132 men, under the command of Major Prince. The sea was calm, the weather fine, and everything indicated a speedy resumption of her voyage. The vessel had touched at Crescent City for the purpose of landing passengers, freight, mail and express matter. After the mail and express matter had been landed, it was perceived that an unusual quantity of smoke was issuing from the vessel, and many were the conjectures respecting the cause. But conjecture was soon solidified into the certainty that the vessel was on fire, and a scene of indescribable excitement ensued, both on shore and at sea. Lighters, boats, and canoes dotted the bay and surrounded the ill-fated vessel; those on shore could see that the crew and soldiers on board were making almost superhuman exertions to master the threatened calamity.

The report of Capt. T. J. Wright, owner of the vessel, published in the Crescent City Herald, states that "in about 15 minutes after anchoring discovered large quantities of smoke issuing from the coal bunkers, when the cry of "fire," was given No flame could be seen, but volumes of smoke and gas enveloped the vessel so completely that it was utterly impossible to go below, and the exact location of the fire could not be ascertained. Having a large number of soldiers on board, in addition to the crew of the vessel, all the pumps were manned and every exertion was made to save the ship. The officers and crew of the vessel performed their duty faithfully; working incessantly amid the flames and suffocating gas and smoke, never leaving their posts for a moment, until they were requested to do so and take to the boats. The fire was purely accidental, and is supposed to have originated in the coal bunkers from spontaneous combustion."

All the soldiers who could be spared from the vessel were soon sent ashore, and in about 30 minutes after the fire was first discovered the ship was run aground in the shallow water about one hundred and fifty yards from shore.

Fire, and especially a fire on board a ship, will arouse all the energy and enlist the aid of any people. The citizens of Crescent City were eager to save the burning vessel, and with wonderful rapidity and energy buckets, ladders, ropes, and everything deemed useful were sent on board. At times it seemed that the fiery element must yield to such persistent and united efforts; but the dense smoke gradually deepened and darkened, the efforts on board became feebler on account of the impossibility of men maintaining their positions, and a sheet of clear flame that tore through the black sky proclaimed the triumph of the destroyer.

Seeing no hopes of saving the ship, the crew and citizens who had fought the fire so gallantly, now left the vessel to her fate. The greedy flame fed eagerly, and on Monday morning a charred, smouldering and hideous skeleton was all that remained of the steamer America. Thus ended the career of a vessel almost new, and by far the most efficient steamer that in early days sailed the Northern Pacific.

On the destruction of the steamer becoming certain, the City Council convened, and appointed Major Wendell and

S. G. Whipple a committee to wait upon the owner and commander, and to tender to them, their officers, passengers and crew the hospitalities of the city. This act on the part of the citizens showed both courtesy and kindness, but some circumstances connected with the catastrophe reflect no credit upon any of the parties concerned. It is said that the boatmen of the place made exorbitant charges for their services in saving goods from the vessel, and that the soldiers, as soon as they were landed, commenced a pilfering war on the citizens' pork and poultry. Perhaps it is only charitable to suppose that the poor fellows were hungry, and had no felonious intentions when they committed these depredations; but some doubt is thrown on this supposition by the following toast, proposed by one of the Company on the Fourth of July:

"The Gallant 21st---Set them before Sebastopol, and if they cannot conquer, they will steal it!"

The America was built by Wm. H Brown, New York, in 1853, and registered 923 tons. She was brought around Cape Horn by Capt. Mitchell, arriving at San Francisco in 1854. She was there bought by J T. Wright and employed in the coast trade, the principal portion of the time running to Crescent City. The vessel was valued at $140,000, and was uninsured.

Sometime after the fire the hulk was examined and it was thought that it would pay to tow it to San Francisco, where the vessel could be rebuilt. Accordingly, the steamer Goliah took the hulk of the America in tow, and towed it safely until off Point Reyes, where she experienced heavy weather and broke the hawser, thus sending the unwieldy hulk adrift. Every effort was made to regain her, but without success, and the last seen of the America she was full of water, the sea breaking clear across.

As the first rays of sunlight flashed on the waters of the bay on the morning of the Fourth of July, 1855, the roar of three brass cannon ushered in the dawn of the eightieth birthday of our independence. These cannon had been recovered from the wreck of the steamer America, and were placed on Battery Point, a rocky strip of land forming the left hand horn of the crescent shaped beach, and elevated above the ocean some twenty or twenty-five feet. Here, in place of a light-house there was a large lantern fixed on the top of a stout pole; this pole was at regular intervals pierced with holes through which projecting pins were driven, forming a sort of primitive stairway to the Fresnel light above. Near this pole, on a spot commanding a view of the whole town, the cannon were placed, and throughout the day their hoarse voices proclaimed the independence and patriotism of the people. A procession was formed and marched through the principal streets, including the detachment of U. S. Infantry under command of Major Henry Prince, the Crescent Hook and Ladder Company, and the local military companies. W. A. Hamilton was Grand Marshal, J. J. Arrington and F. E. Weston, Assistants. The Declaration of Independence was read by J. B. Rosborough, and the oration was delivered by Jno. P. Haynes.

On the 5th of September a general election was held throughout the State, which was of special importance to this county. It had long been a disputed question as to which town in the county was entitled to be the county seat. When Klamath county was created Trinidad was the county seat. It was afterwards removed to Crescent City, but the people living on the Klamath river were still dissatisfied, and urged that the county seat be removed to Orleans Bar. This place, about 150 miles from Crescent City, is situated in the midst of a mining district on the Klamath river. At the general election above mentioned Orleans Bar was declared by the votes of the people to be the county seat "from and after the 4th day of December, A. D. 1855."

Owing to heavy snows, blocking up the trails, the winter of 1855-6 was very dull, and Crescent City wore an almost deserted look. But with the advent of spring came a general revival of trade; the streets were again enlivened by the jingling tramp of trains, the sidewalks encumbered with packages, and the stores resounded to the bustling, hurrying voices of traders and packers. The rate of freight from San Francisco to Crescent City was, with but little variation, $12 per ton on sailing vessels, and $20 per ton on steamers. Passage, in cabin, $40; in steerage, $20. The pack trains received from 2 to 5 cents per pound for carrying freight to various places in this county and Southern Oregon. The express companies were doing a large business, from $150,000 to $200,000 in gold dust passing through Crescent City during the business season of the year.

On March 1st, 1856, Crescent City was excited when a party of six men returned from the mouth of Rogue river, and confirmed the reports of certain depredations and massacres by the Indians previously received. On account of the war on Rogue river, the Indians all along the coast were greatly excited, and those in the vicinity of Crescent City and Smith's river spoke continually of the Indians above intending to come down and drive off the whites. Some went so far as to intimate that in a "few sleeps" all would be over with the whites.

The Indians on Chetco river had become refractory, and were threatening the whites. The Indians in the immediate vicinity were very much frightened, and represented to the whites that they were in great danger of being annihilated by the Rogue River Indians. Under these circumstances the citizens had made arrangements, in conjunction with Capt. Jones, U S. A , who was then stationed at Crescent City with a company of 50 men, to patrol the streets during nights. Capt. Jones assigned half of his command to this duty, while the other half were ordered to proceed to Smith's River Valley.

A FALSE ALARM. 41

Expectation was on tiptoe, and a feeling that something was going to happen pervaded the community. The most unfounded rumors were circulated during the excitement, and the most absurd reports were taken for certainties. Several citizens were reported killed, who in reality had not seen an Indian. All the houses in Smith's River Valley were reported to be in flames, and 300 hostile savages scattered over the valley. And notwithstanding that no band of hostile Indians had been seen within twenty miles of the town, rumor had spread the report on the other side of the mountains that Crescent City had been totally destroyed by an incendiary fire.

All the brick stores in town were used to shelter those who could not face the enemy. The brick building on Second street erected the year before by J. J. Friedman & Co., received probably the largest share of these transient tenants. No less than 30 ladies and 15 or 20 children were there congregated, awaiting and dreading the attack of the Indians.

The streets wore a martial appearance. The "boys in blue" were to be met with at every corner—saloon — while companies of gallant Volunteers patroled the streets and declared that they were one and all prepared to die "for their country's good." Dwelling houses and stores were transformed into armed citadels, and every householder could truly say that his house was his castle.

Although the terror of the inhabitants was real and not feigned, several amusing incidents occurred during the excitement. Numerous unfounded reports made Uncle Sam's "boys" wish they were in some other part of the world, and caused the bold Volunteers to fortify themselves with "Old Rye," or to "screw up their courage to the sticking point" by a "stone-fence" or an "eye-opener."

On one occasion, a practical joke was perpetrated on a prominent citizen, causing considerable merriment at the time, and securing several "treats" to "the boys."

It seems that J. F. Wendell and several others were assembled in a certain bar-room, and were discussing the probability of an attack by the Indians, Wendell contending that the danger was great and a fight inevitable. While they were thus discussing the question, some one of a waggish turn of mind affixed a smoked salmon to Wendell's coat tails, who, all unconscious of the act, walked down the street and into the saloon of Arrington & Co. Standing with his back to the stove, the salmon soon began to get warm, and the odor from its scorching sides assailed the nostrils of the unsuspecting Wendell.

The Indians on this coast live mostly on salmon, and consequently bear always with them an unpleasant fishy smell. Therefore it is not surprising that when the salmon affixed to his coat-tails began to fill the room with its odor, Wendell excitedly shouted, "Indians, by gosh!" and rushed from the room in search of his trusty rifle.

On Friday morning, March 5th, before daylight several farmers and residents of Smith's River Valley arrived in hot haste in the city. They reported, that on the day previous their scouts had informed them of the approach of the Indians; that every house along the coast above Smith's River was in flames; and finaly, that but a few hours would remain to the settlers to bring their families to a place of security. It was already dark on the evening of Thursday when they yoked up their oxen and hitched up four teams, loaded wtth their families and a few household articles. After crossing Smith's River their way was for a distance of four or five miles through a dense redwood forest, which made the dark night still darker, and made it necessary to pilot each team by a lantern. The road was new and rough, and after a variety of inci dents almost inevitable to such a trip, the party reached the opening at the head of Elk Valley, and there halted at the place of J. Y. Valentine.

From this place some of the men started on horses to

Crescent City, which, as before mentioned, they reached before daylight on Friday morning.

As the day broke, the bell on the Truck House of the Crescent Hook and Ladder Company rang out its clear notes for a call of the citizens, and a short time afterwards Capt. Jones started with a portion of his men and a number of Volunteers out to Smith's River Valley. At a second meeting during the forenoon, J B. Rosborough was appointed Commander for the purpose of directing the means for the repulsion of the Indians, and sundry parties were sent out in different directions to scour thoroughly the neighborhood.

While all this was going on, the report was brought in, between two and three o'clock in the afternoon, that the Indians in large numbers, and well mounted, had been seen but three miles back of the town, and that they would be on the spot in less than an hour.

The successive arrivals of friendly or inoffensive Indians from the neighboring rancherias, formed an episode in the events of the day, adding fuel to the intense excitement pervading the community. These Indians, partly on the representations of the whites, and partly of their own accord, put themselves under the protection of the whites, and were removed to the island on which the light-house is now situated. They were understood to confirm the reports previously received; but afterwards it turned out to be another proof, of how much oftener the whites misunderstood than comprehended the meaning of the red man.

Evening drew near, and the town was hushed in expectancy. Every moment the listening ear was strained to catch the stealthy tread of the red-skin; but the night wore away, and still no savage war-cry had been heard, and when morning broke, the inhabitants were gratified to find that their scalps yet remained in their proper positions.

Then followed explanations: A drove of mules in charge of some Mexicans on their way to Crescent City had been taken for a band of hostile Indians; other causes of alarm were disposed of by similar developments, and on the return of the several scouting parties during the day, it was ascertained that no hostile band had crossed or even as much as reached so far south as Smith's River. Thus the panic ended, and the people once more resumed their accustomed manner of life. Guards were, however, placed during the nights for some time afterwards, and the Indians confined on the island were not removed for several days. The number of Indians confined on the island, as shown by the rations issued on the 2d of March, 1856, were: Smith's River, 179; Lagoon, 58; Ottegon, Chacha, Kobpay. Neckel, 79; Total, 316.

In the Crescent City Herald of April, 1856, I find the first record of a theatre in Crescent City "Not one of those gorgeous palaces, within whose walls the people in large and crowded cities lounge away their leisure hours, but still a theatre, within brick walls, with a neat stage, scenery, footlights, and all the most indispensible paraphernalia of a Thespian temple," was erected in Crescent City. The theatre is situated in Darby's brick building on Front street, and is capable of seating comfortably 200 persons. On the opening night, the "Crescentonian Dramatic Club" presented "for the first time in Crescent City" the popular drama of "The Toodles," and the evening's entertainment concluded with the laughable farce of "Paddy Miles, the Limerick Boy."

The population of Klamath county in 1856 was estimated as follows: Happy Camp, mining population, 100; Indian Creek, 450; other localities down to the mouth of Salmon River, 250; Salmon River, 1200; Smith's River Valley and Redwood Diggings, mining and farming population, 200; Crescent City, 800; Total, 11,700.

During the summer of 1856 business at Crescent City,

owing to continued Indian difficulties in Oregon, was almost at a standstill. The town was filled with idle miners, who had been forced to leave their claims through fear of the Indians. But in other parts of the county, where the consequences of the Indian troubles were not so severely felt, trade was better, and the miners were still working their claims with profit.

Orleans Bar, the new county seat, was the scene of unusual activity. Hundreds of pack mules passed through the place, destined for the upper Klamath and Salmon. Traders were driving a brisk business, miners were doing well, several new buildings were in course of construction, and competition among the business men ran very high. Goods were plenty and cheap, and good living could be had at a lower rate than at any other place on the coast.

Mines were also discovered in the Bald Hills, about six miles from Crescent City, and during the summer the miners there went to great expense in sinking shafts, building flumes, etc. A town was laid out and named Vallardville, after a prominent French citizen, A. Vallard. A company from San Francisco were operating at this place with hydraulic power, probably the first attempt of the kind ever made in the county.

At the 2d session of the 33d Congress an appropriation was made for the erection of a light-house at Crescent City. The sum appropriated was $15,000. A site was selected for the structure in June of the same year.

The first difficulty between the whites and the Chinese occurred in the latter part of June. A company of Chinese had about nine months before purchased a claim on the North Fork of Salmon River of a party of white men. They worked it without much success until the latter part of June, when they struck rich pay dirt, and the parties who had sold it to them, discovering that they (the Chinese) were making money, jumped the claim. The Chinamen sued the white men and recovered judgment for the possession of the claim. The Sheriff of the county proceeded under the judgment and put them in possession of it, and thinking all was right, returned to Orleans Bar. As soon as he had left, the same parties again jumped the claim, and drove the Celestials off. The local officers summoned a posse of citizens to reinstate the Chinamen, but were resisted by the party claiming possession, whereupon they opened fire upon them, killing one man. The rest of the jumping party were arrested by the citizens, and held to answer for their misconduct.

Whether they were punished or not the records do not show; but ten chances to one they were not, for justice in Klamath county, in districts remote from Crescent City, especially, was administered in the rudest and most primitive way. The Justices of the Peace, as a rule, knew more of "bean poker" than of Blackstone, and it was seldom that their decisions were given according to the law and evidence.

To illustrate the scenes which often occurred in these courts of justice, the following is related of a certain Justice's court. It must be premised that the Justice was noted for being irritable and passionate, and consequently, that the "boys" were in the habit of playing jokes upon him.

The defendant, who was brought up for breaking furniture, etc., in a house of rather delicate reputation, had made himself particularly obnoxious to the Justice by his practical jokes. The scene is given as it is said to have occurred, and readers are advised as all pious people should do, to skip the "cuss" words.

The defendant is brought into Court, whereupon, the Justice rising and arranging his spectacles to give him a better view, addresses him, "Well, you d——d long, slab-sided scoundrel, you're here, are you? I have been looking for you a long time, and now I've got you."

Counsel for the prisoner----"If the Court please, I appear

as counsel for the defendant, and would request that you address yourself to me."

Justice----"You be d——d; you must be a blacker hearted villian than he is to come here backing him up in such performances as this."

Counsel---"But, Uncle Robert, you must not decide this case without hearing it. You must have some proof."

Justice----Proof, h--l, haint I been there myself?"

It is needless to add that the defendant was committed for trial.

At another time the prosecuting attorney in a certain case went on to state, "That on such a night, at such a place, in such a county and State, Ben Strong did, in a quiet game of "keards" called euchre, with Joe Short, with malice aforethought and evident intention to rob, steal and swindle, 'turn up' a point more than he had made, thereby unlawfully taking the plaintiff's money."

Ben was also accused of "renigging." Two witnesses were examined as to the character of the opposing parties. Each of the attorneys made a speech and put the case in as strong a light as possible. Then came the "charge:"

"Gentlemen of the jury," commenced the Squire very gravely, "the pints in this here case, like angels visits are few and far betwixt. The Court knows nothing about euchre, and never did, but she knows a few about law, gentlemen of the jury The Court has went through Blackstone, on law, twice, and she has read Snugg's 'seven-up;' and, gentlemen of the jury, she has picked up a good many pints on 'poker'; but she aint nowhere in 'euchre,' and never was. But, gentlemen of the jury, the Court thinks she understands the pints in this case. Ben Strong and Joe Short they played at ten dollars ante, and Ben he won. Will you, gentlemen of the jury, fine Ben for winning? Who wouldn't like to win? Not even the Court herself. But you kin do as you please about it. Then the 'opposit' attorney says that Ben he cheated.

But, gentlemen of the jury did he prove that pint? No, he didn't begin to do it. Ben Strong plays a fair game at 'keards.' The Court has played 'old sledge' and 'whiskey poker' with Ben for the last two years, and he never catched him stocking the papers or turning the Jack from the bottom. But, gentlemen of the jury, you kin do as you please with Ben. The pints in the case, then, gentlemen of the jury, are, first: Ef you find that Ben Strong won Joe Short's money, it is clear that Ben hilt the best keards. Second: Ef you find that Joe lost his money, it is clear that Joe was in d——d bad luck. These, gentlemen of the jury, are all the pints in the case, and you kin retire——and don't be out long, for Ben is going to treat the whole court."

The jury, without leaving their seats rendered a verdict of "not guilty," after which the winning side, headed by the Court, adjourned to a saloon to imbibe. The "opposit" side, headed by Joe Short, left in disgust.

The Board of Supervisors of Klamath county met at Orleans Bar, the county seat, on the first Monday in August, and found that the affairs of the county were in a very bad condition. The Treasurer's books had not been properly made up, and according to the books of the Auditor, a large amount of money had been unaccounted for by the Sheriff. In view of these facts, the Board refused to levy any county tax for that year. The Sheriff had already reported that no property taxes had been collected for the past year.

All this may have been very pleasing to the tax payers, but it was certainly the means of involving the county in a maze of financial difficulties, which it required years to set right.

New and rich mines were discovered on Elk Creek, a stream which empties into the Klamath about one half a mile below Happy Camp. Men were rushing there from all points——numbers having even left the far famed Scott's

Bar. It was estimated that three hundred men were at work, and none of them making less than from $10 to $20 per day. The diggings were very extensive, in fact the whole surrounding country so far as it had been prospected proved to be rich.

In December the Crescent City Plank Road and Turnpike Company perfected their preliminary organization by electing W. A. Hamilton President of the Company; T. S. Pomeroy, Secretary; Henry Smith, Treasurer. Three gentlemen were selected to examine and report the most favorable route for a wagon road. Two years before a company had been formed to construct a wagon road from Crescent City to Illinois Valley, and a survey was made. A large portion of the stock had been taken, when the derangement of business caused by the failure of Adams & Co., Page, Bacon & Co., and many other San Francisco houses of less importance, caused an abandonment of the project.

The new company was formed with the same end in view, but with the advantage of having a new route, over which a road could be built for much less money than over that selected by the old company. The estimated cost of the new road was $50,000, and the estimate of revenue expected to be derived from it was $40,000 a year.

The Legislature of 1857-8 passed a bill providing for the division of Klamath county, and for the creation of the new county of Del Norte. It was first named "Buchanan," but the Committee on Counties and County Boundaries, to whom was referred a bill to establish the new county and define its boundaries, reported it back with the amendment, the name of the county, "Buchanan," be struck out and that "Del Norte" be inserted in its stead.

Mr. Cofforth moved to amend the Committee's amendment by striking out "Del Norte" and inserting "Alta."

Mr. Merritt suggested "Altissima," as it was the farthest county north.

Mr. Cosby suggested " Rincon."

Mr. Westmoreland moved to strike out "Del Norte" and insert " Del Merrit."

The question being taken on these amendments, they were all lost, and after a little more sparring, the amendment " Del Norte " was substituted for " Buchanan," by a vote of 14 to 6, and the bill passed.

It located the seat of Justice at Crescent City, and ordered an election held in May, 1857, for the election of county officers. For Senatorial purposes Del Norte was attached to Klamath, and for Judicial purposes to the 8th Judicial District. The bill also provided that Del Norte pay one third of the indebtedness of Klamath county, and that it was to issue bonds therefor, bearing ten per cent. per annum interest, to Klamath county. Twenty per cent. of the taxes and other monies received by the Treasurer of Del Norte was ordered to be set aside as a sinking fund for the redemption of said bonds; and the sum arising from this twenty per cent. was to be appropriated annually to the redemption of said bonds. The Board of Supervisors of Del Norte county were authorized to levy a special tax, not to exceed twenty-five cents on each one hundred dollars of valuation of taxable property in said county; the fund arising from said special tax to be applied, in addition to the twenty per cent. above mentioned, to the liquidation of the debt due to Klamath county.

The boundaries of Del Norte county were declared to be as follows: " Commencing at a point in the Pacific Ocean. three miles from shore, on 42d parallel of north latitude, and running thence southerly three miles from shore to a point one mile south of the mouth of Klamath River; thence easterly, on a line parallel with said Klamath River, to a point one mile south of the mouth of Blue Creek; thence in a north-easterly direction to the summit of the Siskiyou Mountains; thence in an easterly direction, following the ridge that divides the waters of Clear Creek from the waters of Dillon's Creek, to the Klamath River, at a point equi-distant from the mouth of said Dillon's Creek and the mouth of said Clear Creek; thence across Klamath River, and in an easterly and northerly direction to said Klamath River, at the head of the canon, (said canon being about five miles above the mouth of Indian Creek, and between Eagle Ranch and Johnson's Ranch,) following the ridge of the mountains, and heading the waters that flow into said Klamath River, on the south side, between the two points last beforementioned; thence crossing the river, and in a northerly direction following the ridge dividing the waters that flow into the river above from the waters that flow into the river below the place of crossing, to a point on the 42d parallel of north latitude, due north from the head of said canon; and thence west to the place of beginning."

As may be seen from the above, the boundaries embraced all the country on both sides of the Klamath River as high as a point five miles above the mouth of Indian Creek, and as far down that river as a point half-way between Clear Creek and Dillon's Creek, taking in Elk Creek and the mining country thereabouts; in fact including the points of Happy Camp, Elk Creek, Wingate's Bar, Spanish Bar, Clear Creek, Indian Creek, Forks of Smith's River, and Crescent City and the adjoining country.

U. B. Freaner, J. T. Bayse, Peter Darby, R. B. Morford and P. H. Peveler were appointed a Board of Commissioners to divide the county into three Supervisor Districts, to designate election precincts, to appoint officers of election, to receive the returns, and to issue certificates of election to those entitled to the same.

The month of April, 1857, brought the heaviest immigration to Del Norte that had ever been known during the same length of time. Over 450 passengers were landed at the port of Crescent City within three days.

On Monday, May 4th, 1857, the election for county officers for the new county of Del Norte took place, and the officers elected were: County Judge, F. E. Weston; County Clerk, Ben. Reynolds; Sheriff, N. Tack; District Attorney, Jno. P. Haynes; Treasurer, E. Y. Naylor; Assessor, Solon Hall; Coroner, Jasper Houck; Surveyor, D. C. Lewis; Public Administrator, Jno. T. Boyce. The Supervisors elected were: First District, Wm. Saville; 2d, Ward Bradford; 3d, P. H. Peveler.

The Democratic party in Del Norte county was first organized at the Excelsior Saloon, Crescent City, May 16th, 1857. Jno. P. Haynes, on behalf of a Committee of three appointed to select a County Committee, submitted the names of the following persons to form such County Committee: Crescent City, T. S. Pomeroy, Pat McManus and Peter Darby; Smith's River Valley, Isaac Warwick; Indian Creek, P. H. Peveler; Happy Camp, Mr. Lippard; Klamath River, R. Humphreys.

Pursuant to notice, the stockholders in the Crescent City Plank and Turnpike Company met in the theatre in Crescent City, on the evening of the 4th day of June, for the purpose of electing officers of said Company. W. A. Hamilton was elected President, T. S. Pomeroy, Secretary, and Henry Smith, Treasurer, to hold office for the term of one year. Messrs. J. W. Stateler, John A. Baxter, F. E. Weston, David Price, D. C. Dewis, E. Y. Naylor and J. G. Wall were elected Directors of the Company for one year.

An assessment of $10 on each share of stock was levied, and Marney & Davis, of Jacksonville, Jacob Mendenhall, of Illinois Valley, and J. R. Sloan, of Kirbyville, were appointed agents to collect the same in their respective vicinities. Through the untiring exertions of the President, W. A. Hamilton, all the stock in the enterprise had been subscribed for, to the amount of $50,000.

The summer of 1857 found Del Norte county in a prosperous condition. And in taking a retrospective view of their situation the people of Del Norte had much to congratulate themselves upon, and had good reason to expect a great increase in population, business and wealth during the years to come. The division of Klamath county had been accomplished and the new county of Del Norte created; and above all, the determination shown by the Judicial officers of the new county to punish, and thereby prevent crime, augured a new era in the administration of county affairs, and an improvement in the moral tone of the community. Another object, the building of the wagon road across the mountains, could now be considered as certain of success.

During the months of March, April and May, the first business months of the year, there were landed at Crescent City 1278 tons of freight, and 1717 passengers. And the above may be taken as a fair criterion of the average business of the town in 1857.

The mines were also paying as well if not better than formerly. The miners on the Klamath were making good wages. On Indian Creek the miners were making an ounce per day to the hand.

The Crescent Hook and Ladder Company gave their third annual ball on July 3d. There was nothing remarkable about the ball, except the fact that the price of tickets was placed at $10 each; which would certainly be a remarkable occurrence in these days.

The Democratic Convention to nominate a Senator from this district, which was then composed of the counties of Del Norte, Klamath and Siskiyou, met at Happy Camp on the 29th of July, 1857, and organized by electing Jno. P. Haynes, of Del Norte, President, and R. Haden, of Siskiyou, Secretary. The number of votes allowed each county was as follows: Siskiyou, ten; Klamath, four; Del Norte, three.

On the first ballot D. J. Colton, of Siskiyou, was nominated unanimously.

Afterwards, the delegates from Klamath and Del Norte went into convention for the nomination of a candidate to represent those two counties in the Assembly, and nominated R. P. Hirst, of Klamath county, for that office.

On Wednesday, September 2, a murder occurred that caused great excitement throughout this county and Southern Oregon, and led to the belief that an organized band of cut-throats and robbers were plying their vocation in this part of the State.

Max. Rothenheim, a prominent merchant of Crescent City, was murdered and robbed in broad daylight on the trail leading from that place to Illinois Valley. The circumstances, as detailed by Mr. Lewis, who was traveling with him at the time, are as follows: Rothenheim and Lewis stopped at Elk Camp (thirty miles from town) on the 1st of September, they being on their way from the mining districts to Crescent City. They took an early breakfast on the morning of the 2d, and started on. They had got about a mile on their way, when Lewis, who was in advance, heard someone order them to "halt," and looking up saw a man standing ahead of them in the trail, masked, and with a shot-gun presented at him. He sang out to Rothenheim to shoot him, and jumped from his horse. As he touched the ground the man fired, and Lewis' horse was struck by several buck-shot. He seized the bridle of his horse and ran down the trail with him some twenty-five yards, when he heard another shot and saw Rothenheim fall. As he fell someone said, "you're safe," and he then saw another man, also masked, and with a revolver. Rothenheim's mule was running, and the first man he saw cried out, "never mind the mule, shoot the man." Lewis' horse had fallen dead and he continued his flight, and by a circuitous route returned to Elk Camp, where he remained until the Express train came along, and accompanied it in to town. On arriving at the scene of the murder they found the dead horse, but could not see anything of the body of Rothenheim, the murdered man.

As soon as the news reached town the excitement was intense, and Coroner Houck and Deputy Sheriff Riley with a party started at once to search for the body. It was found some twenty yards from the trail, where Rothenheim had apparently laid down himself, as his attitude was perfectly easy and natural, and there were no marks of his being taken there by violence. The body had been robbed of everything valuable. The amount of money Rothenheim had is not known, but it is known that he had made some collections in the mines, and that he also had about $700 belonging to another person.

The body was taken to Crescent City, where an inquest was held, after which it was shipped to San Francisco for interment. At the inquest to enquire into the cause of the death the following verdict was found:

"The jury empaneled to enqire into the cause of Max Rothenheim's death find as follows, viz: That the said Max Rothenheim came to his death by a gun-shot wound inflicted by some person or persons to the jury unknown. That said killing was committed in the county of Del Norte, State of California, about one mile from Elk Camp, on the road from Crescent City to Illinois Valley, and occurred on the 2d day of September, 1857. We are also of the opinion that the crime of murder was committed with the design of robbery, by two or more persons, and we have reason to suspect Bill Judd and accomplices of the perpetration of the crime."

Many different theories were advanced as to how and by whom the murder of Max Rothenheim was committed, but through all the contradictory opinions expressed, one conviction forced itself into the minds of all—that this portion of the State, which had before been free from the drepredations of the gangs of highwaymen who had infested other parts of it, could no longer be exempt from their rascally deeds. It was thought by many that an organized band of robbers and murderers had their haunts in Northern California and Southern Oregon, and that these bands had friends and agents everywhere. That all parties coming to Crescent City from the interior, who were known or supposed to have money with them, were watched there can be no question. Besides the murder of Rothenheim on the trail, there had been, within a week previous to it, two robberies committed, one in Crescent City and one in Smith's River Valley. Men known to be bad and desperate characters had been seen in various parts of the county, though fortunately perhaps for themselves, they did not remain.

Ely Judd and Bill Judd, two brothers, were supposed to be the murderers, and one of them, Ely, was arrested by the citizens of Happy Camp and kept a prisoner for three days. He then managed to make his escape. He was followed some distance up the river by Henry Doolittle and others, but was not recaptured at the time.

The "Metropolitan Theatrical Company," from San Francisco. made their first appearance in Crescent City on Monday evening, September 28th, 1857. The plays selected were "Perfection" and "Loan of a Lover." The circumstance making the "Metropolitan's" worthy of notice in these pages is, that among them was one who was destined to receive the homage of the world; whose acting would some day delight and amuse thousands upon thousands of people; whose lightest word and slightest gesture upon the stage would hold countless audiences spell-bound, and bring hundreds of admirers to her feet.

All history has shown that the greatest men and women of any age rose from the lower walks of life, and step by step, mounted the ladder of fame, until they reached the topmost round. And they have sprung from the most unexpected and unlikely places; from hot-beds of vice and crime, they have passed unscathed to a higher and a better life; from the lowest and most degrading surroundings, they have risen to be shining lights in the constellation of dramatic, literary and scientific celebrities. In the words of the poet:

> "All the world's a stage,
> And all the men and women
> merely players;
> They have their exits and
> their entrances,
> And one man in his time
> plays many parts."

And it is not surprising that upon the stage of a small theatre in a far off California town, one of the most celebrated actresses of modern times "made her entrance" into public notice, and laid the foundation for a great success upon the stage.

This member of the "Metropolitan" troupe was no other than the now famous Lotta---whose naive ways, sweet, childish voice, and nimble feet were even then giving promise that she might, with careful training, achieve a high position in her profession. She had already become a capital little actress, but it was on this tour through Northern California and Southern Oregon that she first gained a secure hold on the good-will and admiration of the public. The troupe played through the week in Crescent City to full houses, afterwards leaving for the interior, where they met with equally large and enthusiastic audiences.

The Board of Examiners appointed under the provisions of the Act of the Legislature of 1856-7 dividing Klamath county and creating the new county of Del Norte, consisting of Messrs. Lewis, Peveler, McDonald and Buel, met at Orleans Bar on the third Monday in September, and proceeded to the discharge of their duties. They first went to work to ascertain the indebtedness of Klamath county prior to the 4th day of May, 1857, and finding it impossible to do so in any other way, fixed upon the proceedings of the Funding Commissioners of Klamath county as the basis of said debt, notwithstanding a large number of bills had been audited by the Supervisors of that county since the organization of Del Norte, the most of which were audited at a special term in June, 1857. The whole of this bill was $5,534.85.

It was problematical whether Del Norte was properly responsible for any portion of this amount, in the auditing of which she had no voice; but taking into consideration the distracted condition of the county government of Klamath prior to May, 1857, the death of her Treasurer, the resignation of her Assessor, the default and absconding of her Sheriff, and the necessity that existed of having all claims against her audited before the funding of her debt, the Examiners thought it best to take the amount funded by Klamath as the amount of her debt previous to May 4th, deducting from it, however, the debts incurred by Klamath during the month of May. That amount, making allowances for back licenses collected by Klamath, and also for warrants redeemed by her from her own funds, was in all $26,843.54. This then, was the amount to be divided between the two counties.

The next step was to establish a basis on which to divide it. On this point the words of the Act creating the Board of Examiners were, "and when the amount of indebtedness is so ascertained, they shall determine the amount of said indebtedness to be paid by Del Norte county, taking as a basis the sources of revenue of the two counties." The Del Norte Examiners therefore proposed to take as a basis the sources of revenue of the two counties for the year ending in 1858, taking the licenses for May, June and July, 1857, as the basis for the year.

This apportionment would have resulted as follows: Revenue of Klamath for the year, $10,659.80; revenue of Del Norte, $6,555.75.

At which rate the proportion of Del Norte would have

been a trifle more than one third of the whole debt. To this proposition the Examiners on the part of Klamath dissented, urging as a reason for their dissent, that it was working injustice to them to take into the calculation the revenue derived from Foreign Miner's License. It was urged upon the Klamath Examiners that if the Foreign Miner's License was a source of revenue, they (the Klamath Examiners) were unjust; if it was not a source of revenue their view was correct. And to show how strongly it was relied on as a source of revenue, the fact was mentioned that an adjoining county in Oregon relied entirely upon this tax for the support of her county government, and levied no property tax at all. However, the Klamath Examiners were firm in their refusal, and the Examiners from Del Norte, would accept no other proposition.

The Board then endeavored to agree upon a fifth man to decide the point, but there they failed again, and were compelled to adjourn without accomplishing anything more than the ascertaining the amount of debt to be divided.

As before stated, the whole debt outstanding of Klamath county on the 4th day of May, 1857, of which Del Norte had to pay its portion, was $26,843.54. The Board having failed to divide this, the only thing now to be done under the provisions of the division act, was for the County Auditor of Del Norte to draw his warrant on the Treasurer of said county for one-third of this amount, being $8,948.09. A very nice little sum for Del Norte to have on her back at the commencement of her existence.

Nothing of special interest occurred during the opening months of the year 1858, except the capture of Bill and Ely Judd, two notorious characters who were suspected of having been engaged in the murder and robbery of Rothenheim, the summer before. They were captured near Shasta by the Sheriff of Shasta county, where they were turned over to Deputy Sheriff Riley, of Del Norte, who took them to Crescent City and lodged them in jail.

After being lodged in jail at Crescent City they were searched, and a file made of a piece of steel spring was found on each, concealed in their hats. They had a preliminary examination before Justice Mason, and were committed to await the action of the Grand Jury.

But these desperate men were determined to escape from the clutches of the law, and on Monday evening, February 1st, the citizens were alarmed by the cry that the prisoners had escaped. It appeared that Deputy Sheriff Liddle and the jailer, Mr. Sykes, had just taken the prisoner's supper to them, and as usual, had removed the irons from their wrists that they might eat with more ease. They had finished their supper, Mr. Liddle had replaced the irons on Ely Judd, and was about doing so on Jack (a man in jail for robbery) when Jack struck him a severe blow on the head, having one hand-cuff on. Mr. Liddle stepped back, to get out of the way of the irons, but Jack struck him several times on the head with them, cutting it badly. Bill Judd at the same time knocked Sykes down the steps, and he and Jack made a rush out of the door, they having previously cut the chains which bound the irons on their legs. Ely made no attempt to run. Jack did not get far, for Mr. Liddle, cut and bleeding as he was, and compelled to hold on to the railing for support, fired two shots at him, one of which took effect, and he was soon secured and brought back, badly wounded. In the meantime Bill Judd made a run for the woods back of the jail and was soon out of sight, it being then nearly dark. Several parties went in pursuit, but without success. Sheriff Tack offered a reward of $500 for Judd, and he was finally captured on the Klamath by four soldiers stationed on the reservation, and again taken back and lodged in jail.

Many complaints were made during the spring of 1858

in regard to the management of the Klamath Indian Reservation, and people were beginning to think that it was something of a humbug. It was supposed to have been established for the purpose of collecting the Indians upon it, and maintaining them there, teaching them to cultivate the soil, and for that purpose a great deal of government money had been spent every year. But instead of answering the purpose for which it was intended, the Reservation was notoriously mismanaged, and the Indians were prowling around when and where they pleased.

Crescent City was full of them; they were all over it at nights, they were sleeping in buildings in all parts of it---and it was in constant danger of being set on fire by their carelessness. It was the duty of the Government to get all the Indians on the reservation and keep them there, and as it was then being conducted, it was a reservation only in name. And, as usual in such cases, the blame could not be traced to any one whose duty it would become to afford relief.

The Crescent City Plank Road and Turnpike Company completed their road in May, 1858, and the first stage over the whole length of the road left Crescent City on the 19th of that month. The first stage line was established by McClellan & Co. and P. J. Mann, and a tri-weekly stage was run from Crescent City to Sailor Diggings, connecting there with the stage line for Jacksonville, Yreka, and intermediate places.

Fraser River became the new Eldorado toward which all eyes were turned during the summer of 1858, and Del Norte suffered severely from the constant drain upon her population which ensued. The Fraser River mines were said to be immensely rich, and many fabulous stories were told in regard to the great fortunes made there. The fever raged with the utmost intensity. On the street, in saloons and billiard halls, in the bar-rooms of hotels, in public halls and in private circles, the all-absorbing and only topic of conversation was the Fraser River mines. Crescent City presented alternately an empty or crowded appearance as steamers were just leaving or just arriving to take away the numbers that were flocking in from the interior to take passage on them.

The saloons presented much the appearance of '54, being filled with miners playing billiards and cards, and drinking poor whiskey. Gambling tables groaned under their burdens of coin and gold-dust, and the miner's money seemed to have caught the prevailing excitement, so rapidly did it change from one pocket to another.

But Crescent City was not the only part of the State which suffered from this excitement. Other places on the Coast became almost depopulated. Trinidad had but six inhabitants left, and numbers were leaving Humboldt, from which bay, in addition to the steamers, two sailing vessels departed with passengers for the North. Kerbyville had "gone in," Jacksonville was thinning off rapidly, and miners were fast leaving the different creeks and diggings on the Klamath.

All this had a serious and detrimental effect on the business and prosperity of the county---in fact, it was the first swash of the wave of adversity which afterwards broke over Del Norte.

The Indians living on Smith's River imitated the oft-repeated example of the whites, and in May, 1859, invoked the aid of Judge Lynch to help one of their brethren to "shuffle off this mortal coil." An Indian belonging to the Yontocket tribe had murdered one belonging to the Smith's River tribe, without provocation. He was taken to Crescent City, when the tribe of the murdered Indian, with Ilas, its chief, and the brethren of the victim, took the Indian out on Battery Point, and hung him at the same spot where the murderers of French had been executed four years before. The brother of the prisoner fastened the rope around his neck himself with every appearance of heartfelt satisfaction. They were not adebts, however, in the white man's mode of punishing criminals, and made three several attempts before they finally succeeded in extinguishing the life of the unfortunate brave. The Indians were not interfered with in any manner by the whites, although a large crowd had collected at the scene of execution.

The Legislature of 1858--9 appointed Commissioners to apportion the Funded Debt of Klamath county, and the interest thereon, between the counties of Klamath and Del Norte. This question had long been a bone of contention between the two counties, and several attempts to settle the matter had been made without success. The Act appointing the Commissioners provided and specified that the revenue of seven months of the year, namely, from June 1st, 1857, to January 1st, 1858, should be the basis of settlement.

The Commissioners, W. M. Buel, on the part of Klamath county, and Ben. F. Dorris, on the part of Del Norte county, declined to act in the premises, alleging as a reason, that, in their opinion, a just and equitable settlement could not be made according to the provisions of said Act. In their report to the Board of Supervisors of Del Norte county, they stated, that upon an examination of the statements furnished them by the Auditors of the two counties showing the net revenues of both, they found that seven months taken as a basis would work greatly to the prejudice of Klamath county. They therefore proposed, after a due consideration of all the circumstances attending the embarrassed condition of affairs, to take the revenue of the first year, namely, from May 4th, 1857, to May 4th, 1858, as the basis of settlement. The apportion ment on this proposition was as follows: Joint debt of Klamath and Del Norte counties, as ascertained from the books of Funding Commission. $31,986.54; amount of revenue collected in both counties from May 4th, 1857, to

May 4th, 1858, $14,667,69; apportionment of the debt according to the above basis---Klamath county, $20,307.00; Del Norte county, $11,679.54; interest to be calculated to the 11th of June, 1859.

On the 7th of July, 1859, the Judds, who had so long been confined in the county jail, waiting their trial for the murder of Rothenheim, made their escape. This was done by sawing out one side of the iron bars of the window in the rear of the building, and then forcing them around, leaving an aperture through which they made their escape. As far as the county was concerned, it was benefitted by their escape, for they had been living at its expense for nearly two years, and after such a lapse of time their conviction was at least exceedingly doubtful.

About three o'clock on the afternoon of the 9th of the same month, a fire broke out on Front street, near J. The flames spread with great rapidity, and in a very short time the entire block on Front, up to I street, was consumed, with the exception of the two brick buildings on the lower corner. The loss by the fire was about $30,000. The principal sufferers were Wenger & Co., M. J. McNamara. G. Patchin, H. B. Congdon, Mrs. H. Grubler, and the Herald. A few days after the fire the citizens held a meeting and adopted measures towards procuring a fire engine for the town, their late experience having fully demonstrated the necessity for such an article.

The county had again the pleasure of boarding the distinguished individual known as Ely Judd, he being captured near Jacksonville in September and taken back to Crescent City Bill Judd was also captured, in Washington Territory, taken back and lodged in jail at the same place.

The case of the People vs. Judd was tried at the Nov. term of the District Court, and the jury returned a verdict of not guilty, which created a great deal of astonishment among citizens generally.

On motion of the District Attorney, the indictment against the Judds was ordered dismissed by the Court, and they were discharged from custody. And so ended the Judd farce, in which the ends of justice had not been carried out, innocent blood had not been atoned for, and the tax-payers of Del Norte had been saddled with a debt of thousands of dollars.

CHAPTER III.

COPPER MINES----WHAT "HUMBOLDT" DID----DEL NORTE POLI-
TICS IN 1860----THE CLOUDS OF WAR----GREAT
FLOOD OF 1861-2 ---AN INSULT TO
THE FLAG----FROM THE YEAR
1859 TO 1865.

The fact that copper existed in large quantities in Del Norte county had long been known, and in March, 1860, numerous specimens taken out by parties who opened the vein were tested by D. S. Sartwell, Dr. Henry Smith, and others, all of which proved the ore to contain a large per cent. of pure copper. This induced the formation of a company, under the direction of D. C. Gibbs, Geologist, who was one of the discoverers, for the purpose of more thoroughly prospecting the vein, which was well defined, the out-croppings having been easily traced for over a mile.

The vein was first opened at a point about two-thirds up the hills rising back from Smith's River, near Black's Ferry, eight miles from Crescent City, and at an elevation of 500 feet from the river. The existence of copper in this section had been known to many since 1853, but until the spring of 1860 no attempt was made to find the vein or test the quality of the loose pieces occasionally found.

The company mentioned above made several openings to the depth of from 20 to 30 feet along the lead at different points, in order more fully to ascertain the character of the lead and the quality of the ore. The discoveries made by them were enough to prove that the county was rich in various minerals, and all that was needed was the energy to prospect, and continue prospecting, until the hidden treasures of her hills would claim for Del Norte an enviable position among her sister counties.

That great institution, the capital stock of Fourth of July orators and prosy political speakers----the American eagle--- had for several years been soaring over the tree tops in the vicinity of Crescent City, and many attempts were made to capture it; and at last it was taken captive near town by J. Lord, who sent it to San Francisco.

Twenty years ago gambling was a prevailing vice in California, and Del Norte was not an exception. The saloons in every mining camp in the county were the headquarters of "poker sharps" and professional gamblers. And the saloons of Crescent City, especially, were the favorite haunts of those who were eager to stake their honor, reputation and money on a game at cards.

After the business hours of the day were over, the different places of resort presented an interesting commentary on the influence of California life upon all classes of society. The propensity of the early California population to invest in great mining schemes, and risk their all to gain a sudden fortune, had left its impress on those who came after them. Everything was the subject of speculation. Chance entered into every business transaction, and it is not surprising that the same element entered into and composed a part of the pleasures of those whose sole ambition was to make their "pile" and return to "the States."

Night after night, in the principal saloons of Crescent City, the card-tables were surrounded by a motley crowd of gamblers. And these were not confined to the "professionals," or those who made their living by gambling.

Frequently, at the same table the merchant sat opposite the miner, the packer faced the new arrival from the East ready to be "fleeced." Thousands of dollars changed hands in the space of a few hours. Some, calm and cool, lost and won their money with a stoical indifference worthy of a Sphinx; others, feverish and excited, nervously dealt the cards, or eagerly watched every turn in the tide of fortune.

On Sunday evening, May 20th, 1860, a man called "Humboldt" had engaged in a "little game" and had met with bad luck. The cards had turned against him all the evening, and he had lost a large amount of money. However, it so happened that "for ways that are dark, and tricks that are vain" "Humboldt" was peculiar. He was up to several dodges of which the uninitiated had no knowledge, and determining to " stock " a deck of cards, and thereby increase his chances of winning, it is said that he went to a room in the Oriental Hotel with the purpose of secretly "fixing up" the deck. Having a lighted candle in his hand, and being too much under the influence of liquor to heed the danger from fire, a few minutes only had elapsed when flames were seen issuing from the building. The fell destroyer spread rapidly, and in spite of all exertions the entire block was soon consumed. The engine company, Active No. 1, was promptly on hand, but water was scarce and she was finally obliged to take it from the slough on Second street. The citizens were out in a body, and together with the firemen worked hard to save all that was possible. The loss amounted to over $10,000.

The summer of 1860 was attended with great excitement in consequence of new discoveries of copper ledges, and the mines attracted considerable attention in San Francisco and other places. A party of Cornish miners arrived and pronounced the ore they saw here the richest they had ever seen before. The ore was not only rich, it was accessible. Wherever the leads were worked the more positive became the evidence of their value. In consequence the inhabitants of this section of country got the copper fever badly, and were much excited over the new discoveries. In fact, copper was all the rage and all the cry. Oxides, and sulphurets, and casings, and out-croppings were familiar words on the lips of men who a few months before would have been puzzled to define them. At one time there was a regular stampede in Crescent City. The streets were deserted, and the stables were bare of either horse or mule.

A short account of the different claims then located in the county will probably be of general interest, and below will be found the best information in regard to them it has been possible to obtain:

The "Evoca" Company, which was the first one organized, located their mine on the trail leading from Black's Ferry into Illinois Valley, about a half a mile beyond the ferry. The "Excelsior" was situated on the same range of mountains, one mile north of the "Evoca." The "Pacific" was on the same range of mountains, still further, say half a mile, to the northward. The "Del Norte" was located on the left hand side of Myrtle Creek, two and a half miles from Black's Ferry. The "Alta California" was located on what is known as the Low Divide, on the wagon road from Crescent City to Illinois Valley, the lead crossing the road. Next beyond the "Alta California" on the Low Divide was the "Union," on the opposite side of the road from where the "Alta" company were working. Other mines, namely, the "Crescent," "Bamboo," "Mammoth," and the Chaplin and Bradford claims, were located near the Low Divide.

When it is considered that but two months and a half had passed since the first out-croppings had been discovered and tested, and that that short space of time had called all these companies into existence, it will readily appear that the copper mines were not a myth, but something really substantial.

The Crescent City Wharf, the most western improvment of the kind under the American flag, was completed on August 11th, 1860. The whole distance from the shore to the large, flat rock at which it terminated was 1320 feet. It was afterwards continued to the far side of the rock, and then an L was built along that far side, so that vessels could lie head to the sea.

The fall months of 1860 were ca... g... arkable for the great political changes which occur... .. ...vious to 1860 there had been but one political organiz... a in Del Norte —the Democratic party. But the issues then brought before the people were totally different from any that had preceded them. Men recognized the fact that the Union was in danger. The clouds of war, which had been threatening so long, were about to burst over the country. The eloquent words of Patrick Henry were once more ringing through the land: "Gentlemen cry 'peace! peace!' but there is no peace."

No wonder, then, that men who had for years been Democrats, should forsake the party that sought to destroy the Union, and organize into other parties, having for their watchword, "the Union forever," and acknowledging no East, no West, no North, no South, but an indissoluble Union under the Stars and Stripes.

The first sign of any dissatisfaction with the established political organization in Del Norte county was manifested by a call for a Union meeting, for the purpose of organizing for the support of Bell and Everett, for President and Vice-President. A meeting was accordingly held at the Court House in Crescent City on the evening of the 23d of August. N. O. Arrington was called to the Chair, and Ben. F. Dorris was chosen to act as Secretary.

The meeting being called to order, several speeches were made, the Chairman referring to the distracted condition of the country, and urging all Union-loving men to abandon the sectional candidates then before the people, and rally to the standard of Bell and Everett.

Dr. F. Knox addressed the meeting at length, showing forth the great necessity for a thorough and complete organization, and a well directed effort on the part of the Union men throughout the country to make "a long pull, a strong pull, and a pull altogether, to bring the great Ship of State into that quiet harbor where vessels safe without their hawsers ride."

The following Preamble and Resolution, submitted with suitable remarks by Jas. H. Gordon, were then adopted:

"WHEREAS, The times are sadly out of joint, and sectional party strife has run to such excess, as to endanger all the best interests of the country, and even to jeopard the perpetuity of the Union itself; and

"WHEREAS, Our only hope for the prosperity of the country, or the permanency of its institutions lies in a speedy return to the principles and practices of our forefathers; therefore, be it

"RESOLVED, That we most heartily approve the action of the National Union Convention at Baltimore, and the nomination of John Bell, of Tennessee, for President, and Edward Everett, of Massachusetts, for Vice-President, and we now resolve ourselves into a Union Club, styled the Bell and Everett Club of Del Norte county."

Meanwhile, the Republicans and Democrats were not idle. Speeches were made throughout the county by E. G. Hayes, D. C. Lewis and Mr. Bassett on behalf of the Republicans, while the Democratic party was still more numerously represented.

Owing to the split in the ranks of the Democrats caused by the nomination of Stephen A. Douglas and Herschel V. Johnson, in opposition to John C. Breckenridge and Joseph Lane, the party in this county was somewhat demoralized. Jno. P. Haynes, (now Superior Judge of Humboldt county,) was the leader of the Douglas faction in Del Norte, and the Crescent City Herald, edited by T. S. Pomeroy, was the mouth-piece of the supporters of Breckenridge. The most prominent men of the county were Democrats, and consequently both factions of the party were represented by able speakers, who made a spirited canvass of the district.

The Eastern news of the attack on Fort Sumter, and the defence and final surrender by Major Anderson, created a profound sensation among the people of the county, as it did all over the State. And in consequence of the depression and gloom caused by this news, together with the hard times which had preceded it, business was at a standstill, and all trades and professions were feeling the effects of the evil which had come upon the Nation. None of the causes of inflation and business excitement operating in the North and East existed here; therefore, trade and enterprise languished and hid themselves away, and all things partook of the general gloom and fear that pervaded the Union. Men knew not how soon the tread of armed feet might be heard in the Golden State, and neighbors looked askance at each other, as if fearful of one another. Journalism was not an exception, and owing to lack of support the publication of the Crescent City Herald was discontinued and the material removed to Jacksonville, Oregon. True, considerable mining was yet going on, and some goods were being carried across the mountains ----but compared with its former trade, Crescent City had sunk to a very low ebb, and the times were at their hardest.

And from the beginning of the year 1861, a blank of several years in the history of Del Norte occurs, which it is difficult to fill up ---not because of the difficulty in procuring reliable information, but for the reason that few events of interest, except the great flood of 1861-2, transpired.

Del Norte, in common with the rest of the State, was vibrating back and forth between hope and fear, as news arrived of the victory of one side or the other. As people living in perilous times, and surrounded by great and threatening evils, as citizens of a country which was being tossed to and fro upon the angry passions of sectional war-fare, they saw their danger, and were awed by the presence of war. This was no time for business activity, when the life and property of the people were threatened by civil war; this was no time for improvement and development by enterprising men, when the gloomy clouds of war and rebellion hung over them, stretching their dark shadows from East to West, from the Atlantic to the Pacific.

Therefore, it was but natural that everything should relapse into a dull waiting, waiting for the storm to break, waiting for the sun of freedom and union to shine forth in its brightness once more.

The winter of 1861--2 was one of unusual severity. The flood-gates of heaven were opened, the rain poured down in torrents, and fierce gales from the ocean added their terrors to the scene The month of December witnessed the worst of these storms. Rain fell in enormous quantities, until rivulets were transformed into brooks, brooks became rushing rivers, and aided by the wind, the mighty waves of the ocean at high tide forced themselves over drift-wood, bulk heads and breakwater, into the streets of Crescent City, extending in some places as far back as Second street. Huge logs were carried up on the sidewalks, crashing into Front street buildings, breaking windows and doors, and doing other damage. On the beach, the drift-wood was piled up to a great height, whole trees being carried in by the tide. From one end of the beach to the other, huge redwood. spruce and fir trees were piled one upon another in inextricable confusion. It is said that after the tide went out a buggy team was driven on the beach between the drift and the water, and that the pile of drift-wood was so high that people on the streets were unable to see the team. The Crescent City Wharf, which had been built the same year by F. E. Wendell, was crushed by the drift-wood and carried away by the sea. The sea and tide were immense, and had it not been for the piles of drift-wood on the beach in front of town, Crescent City would undoubtedly have been almost totally destroyed by the tide.

But the loss in Crescent City was small when compared with the loss on Smith's River and the Klamath. The surrounding country was flooded by Smith's River, and houses, barns, fences, cattle, etc., went down with the stream, and were carried out to sea or broken to pieces by falling and floating trees. The "oldest inhabitant" had never seen the river so high as it was then; even the Indian, usually so fearless of water, was terrified by the rising tide, and the tribes in the valley removed to the mountains for security from the flood. At Fort Dick, (so called from the fact that the citizens had once built a loghouse there for the purpose of defending themselves against the Indians) over a mile from the bed of the river, large dwelling houses were carried by the flood for a distance of half a mile or more. Buildings on the ranch of Major Bradford, a short distance from the river, were moved from their foundations, and much damage done to other property on the ranch. Near the mouth of the river, a fishery owned by W. H. Woodbury was washed away, together with four hundred barrels of salmon.

At the mouth of the Klamath River, the military station was entirely carried away, all the buildings and much other property being lost.

The company of soldiers stationed at the Klamath, under command of Capt. Stewart, were removed immediately after the flood to Smith's River Valley, where they remained until the summer of 1862, when Camp Lincoln was established. Camp Lincoln was situated in Elk Valley, six miles from Crescent City. Several substantial buildings were erected there, a few of which are standing at the present time. Soldiers were stationed there until 1867, when the station was abandoned and the property sold at auction.

Owing to the unsettled state of affairs, the citizens were fearful of trouble with the Indians, as a large number of them were roaming over the county. For the purpose of gathering these bands together where the controlling and restraining influence of the soldiers could be exercised upon them, the Government leased the large ranch of Major Bradford, in Smith's River Valley, and established thereon an Indian Reservation. It was under the supervision of several men at different times, the first being Capt. Buell. A large number of Indians were on the reservation, and they were kept there until the year 1870. In that year the Indians were removed by Agent Whiting to the Hoopa Reservation, on the Klamath River.

During the time of the Civil War nothing of special importance occurred except what has already been related. Trade was depressed, business enterprise was checked, and everybody were waiting impatiently for the end—when the fate of the Union would be decided. The war feeling ran high, and many bitter animosities were engendered by the war question. The majority of the inhabitants of Crescent City, if not openly expressing themselves in favor of secession and rebellion, at least sympathized strongly with the Confederate cause, and many of them were loud in their denunciations of the Union, and openly expressed their feeling against its perpetuation. Those who remained loyal to the Republic and Republican institutions were by far the lesser number, and they were bitterly opposed by the Confederate sympathizers.

There was a flag-pole in front of Dugan & Wall's Express office, on Front street, from which the flag of the

Union was often flung to the breeze. Not to be outdone by their Republican neighbors, the Democrats erected a flag-pole on Second street, just back of the one on Front street; and it was not unusual to see the flag of the Union waving in close proximity to that of the Southern Confederacy. As the war progressed, the bitter feeling between the Democrats and Republicans grew apace. And at one time, as the Democrats were in such a large majority, it was not considered safe to hoist the Union flag on the arrival of the steamers, especially if they brought bad news of the Confederacy.

On one occasion a steamer arrived, and the emblem of liberty and union was run up the flag-pole in front of Dugan & Wall's Express office. But in a few minutes it was observed that it was hauled down again, and the men at work on the lighters in the bay, noticing this, left their work, marched up to the Express office, and asked Mr. Dugan, who had charge of the flag, why it was hauled down. He replied, "It might cause trouble, if the flag is allowed to remain." The men were not satisfied with this excuse, and finally Dugan took the flag out and threw it down on the side-walk. Willing hands were there to hoist it to the top of the pole,

"And all day long it rose and fell,
On the loyal winds that loved it well."

CHAPTER IV.

WRECK OF THE BROTHER JONATHAN----DISCOVERY OF CHROME---
THE SUNDAY LAW----THE OLD GUARD----BEACH
MINING----A LIVELY EARTHQUAKE----
AND OTHER MATTERS, FROM
1859 TO 1881.

That wide world of waters, the sea, is as full of mystery and wonder to-day as it was two thousand years ago, when navigators thought that to go farther than a certain distance from land would result in inevitable death, and that a hand would be raised in the Western waters, indicating the Ultima Thule beyond which it was folly to venture.

And the superstitious awe with which the sea inspires us, is felt now as strongly as it ever was. We may advance in science, religion, and art; we may be free from the fanaticism of religious enthusiasm; our minds may be stored with scientific knowledge, and clear with the enlightenment of the nineteenth century---but still the mystery and dread of the sea is felt by all, and its superstitions still find a place in the minds of men. That vigorous and thoughtful writer on Nature, John Burroughs, says of the sea:

"It is a wide and fearful gulf that separates the two worlds. The landsman can know little of the wildness, savageness, and mercilessness of nature, until he has been upon the sea. It is as if he had taken a leap off into the interstellar spaces. In voyaging to Mars or Jupiter he might cross such a desert---might confront such awful purity and coldness. An astronomic solitariness and remoteness encompasses the sea. The earth and all remembrance of it is blotted out; there is no hint of it anywhere. This is not water, this cold, blue-black, vitreous liquid. It suggests not life, but death. Indeed, the regions of everlasting ice and snow are not more cold and inhuman than the sea."

And it is this terror which its grandeur and power inspires, that feeds the flame of superstition and awe, and keeps it alive in our minds. Dr. Holland says that "it is curious how superstition springs into life at sea. Of all the monsters that swim the deep or haunt the land, there is none so powerful as this, and none like this that is omnipresent. It can be fought or ignored upon the shore, but at sea it looks up from the green hollows of the waves, and lifts its ghostly hands from every white curl of their swiftly formed and swiftly falling summits. It is in the still atmosphere, in the howling wind, in the awful fires and silences of the stars, in the low clouds and the lightnings that shiver and try to hide themselves behind them. Reason retires before its baleful breath, and even faith grows fearful beneath its influence. It fills the imagination with a thousand indefinite forms of evil, and none are so strong as to be unconscious of its power."

Certainly it is this superstitious feeling that makes tales of the sea so absorbingly interesting when all other subjects grow stale and flat. Would that what follows could be given as an off-spring of the imagination, instead of an account of events which actually transpired.

One summer's day in 1865, a great steamship, freighted with a hundred precious lives, and carrying in her hold goods and treasure valued at four hundred thousand dollars, prepared to start on her trip from San Francisco to the Columbia River. The ship was overflowing with life; officers in gay uniforms were busy in preparing for the start; passengers were bidding farewell to friends and kindred dear. Presently, the last farewells were spoken, the decks were cleared of visitors, the gang-way was hauled in, the fiery heart of the monster began to beat and throb, the wheels revolved----and the steamship Brother Jonathan, freighted with bright hopes and brighter expectations, sailed gallantly out through the Golden Gate in a flood of sunshine, with every prospect of a speedy and prosperous voyage.

Captain DeWolf, shaping his course to the North, sailed far out into the great Pacific—until the Heads grew indistinct and shadowy, and the dark, rugged Farrallones faded away in the blue horizon----until the 30th day of July found the ship with nothing in sight but the bending heavens and the heaving waste of waters.

Everything had passed off smoothly till the morning of the 30th, when the wind increased to a howling nor-wester, lashing the sea into a furious commotion. The ship labored and strained in the angry sea, and it was at last thought best to seek a port of safety. She was then about due west from Point St. George, far out to sea, and out of sight of land. Knowing that the Point would afford shelter from the gale, the Brother Jonathan was headed for Crescent City Harbor, just south of the cape.

And not one of her hundred passengers dreamed of the fate in store for them! No one saw the hand of Death beckoning from the silvery tide. No one heard the voices in the wind and waves claiming them for their own.

Off Point St. George, about four miles from land, a reef, known as St. George Reef, extends for several miles westward into the ocean. It is customary for steamers sailing against a nor-wester, to keep close in shore, inside this reef, in order to keep as much as possible out of the wind, and vessels running down the coast to Crescent City also run inside this reef. The Brother Jonathan was steering on her course for Crescent City, and for some reason was running outside the reef as laid down on the chart. She had made the coast to the north of Point St. George, and was therefore running before the wind, as she was making for the harbor to the south of the Point. She was about four miles off Point St. George, the Quartermaster at the wheel, when suddenly she struck with tremendous power on a sunken rock, with such force that her fore mast went through the hull, her fore-yards resting across the rails. Instantly the deck became the scene of the wildest confusion. The crash was so sudden, so unexpected, so awful, that those on board had scarcely recovered from the shock when they saw that their doom was sealed---the ship was fast sinking into the embrace of the hungry waves, and short time was left to prepare for death.

The pen is impotent to portray, the mind too feeble to imagine the scenes that occurred on the deck of the ill-fated steamer. Women fainted and implored for aid; strong men who had looked death in the face a hundred times, stared with fierce eyes at this watery grave; and all looked to the Captain for the means of safety and delivery. Life-preservers were distributed, two guns were fired in quick succession, and command was given to lower the boats from their davits. No sooner was the first boat in the water, than a frenzied crowd rushed to the side and threw themselves into it in such numbers that it was swamped before it could get clear of the steamer. A second and last boat was launched, which succeeded in clearing the vessel, running before the wind in the direction of Crescent City.

Who can describe that last minute on board the sinking ship; the swooning forms on the deck; the selfish struggles for the means of safety; the wild, longing looks at the land and sky which seemed to mock them; the last farewells, given and received, " when eyes spake love to eyes which ne'er might speak again;" the hands and faces raised imploringly toward the heavens, from whence the sun glared coldly down upon them.

One awful, trembling motion of the ship, one dreadful plunge, and the great steamer, which but an hour before had been the boast and pride of man, went down, with all her treasure, her cunning machinery, and her precious human freight, to sleep in the caves of ocean, until by the agency of nature or of man she shall be lifted from her bed. Those who but a moment before had crowded her decks, felt themselves dragged down, down among whirling eddies that tossed them to and fro, in the midst of falling timbers that crushed and maimed them. And in the struggle in the cold, deadly element, many a pulse stopped beating forever, many a life went out.

The boat which succeeded in clearing the sinking vessel and reaching Crescent City, contained the Third Mate, the Steerage Steward, a Quartermaster, and fourteen others. They arrived at Crescent City about four o'clock in the afternoon of the same day, (July 30th, 1865,) and upon their arrival, boats were immediately manned to proceed to the scene of the catastrophe. They returned on the same evening without being able to accomplish anything, having seen no bodies. Early on the following morning, two boats, under command of Benj. West and Anson Burr, started out to make another effort to save life. But their efforts were all in vain. Nothing was visible in the shape of wreckage or human bodies. On the same evening a boat manned by the Third Mate of the Brother Jonathan, Charles Brown, Charles Patterson and —— Davis, started to Eureka to obtain assistance, but returned before reaching that place. They reported that on their way back they saw portions of the hurricane deck of the steamer drifting by, together with beds, trunks, etc., but saw no bodies. The boat which had swamped on being launched from the steamer, drifted ashore on the beach opposite

Crescent City, and a portion of the upper work of the vessel was afterwards found near Point St. George The heel of her fore mast, 20 or 30 feet long, also went ashore near the same place. A boat went up with two of the crew to within a short distance of Seal Rock, and when they returned they reported that they had seen people on the rock. Other boats were immediately manned and went up to the rock, but on arriving there discovered that the objects supposed to be men were only sea-lions.

A few days afterwards a boat-load went up and tried to discover the place where the steamer went down. The Quartermaster pointed out a rock, a small part of which is visible at low tide, as the one on which she struck. The rock was not on the charts, and had never been known before. It was supposed to be a part of the St. George Reef, and was named "Brother Jonathan Rock."

Nine or ten days after the wreck, the bodies of the victims began to come ashore. Every day three or four bodies would be picked up at sea by the boatmen, and many were washed up on the beach in the vicinity of Crescent City. Horrible discoveries were made in caves and among the rocks. Dead faces showed white from tangled seaweed, wild eyes stared up from shallow pools left by receding tides.

As fast as they were secured, the bodies were taken to Dugan & Wall's ware-house, and an inquest was there held by J. E. Eldredge, Coroner. Forty-five bodies were recovered in the vicinity of Crescent City, and many others were found at different points on the coast between Humboldt Bay and the mouth of Rogue River. The bodies recovered here were buried in the Crescent City cemetery. A number of them were afterwards removed by relatives and friends and taken to other places.

On the body of Mr. Nesbeth, editor of the San Francisco Bulletin, was found a will, which stated that it had been written in the cabin of the steamer just before she went down. Who could help admiring the cool self-possession of a man who could thus, in imminent peril of death, forget his own danger in the thought of those whom he would leave behind him?

The number lost on the Brother Jonathan was between eighty and ninety, and the treasure on board has been estimated at $300,000. Col. Wright, commanding the Pacific Coast Division G. A. R., was on board with a large amount of money, with which to pay off the soldiers in Oregon and Washington Territory, and Wells, Fargo & Company also had a large sum on board. Other sums, belonging to private parties, would have swelled the above estimate to a much larger figure, had their been any means of ascertaining their amount.

The Brother Jonathan, Captain DeWolf, was a sidewheel steamship, about 1000 tons burden, and was one of the oldest steamers on the coast. She was at one time esteemed one of the best boats on the Northern Pacific. Several parties have at different times endeavored to find the sunken steamer, but have thus far been unsuccessful. Old Ocean keeps well its secrets, and it is probable that the lost steamer will forever be hidden from the eye of man. A few articles from the wreck were recovered, and are still preserved in Crescent City. The wheel (which was picked up on the beach a few days after the wreck) is in the possession of Peter Darby; also a bundle of papers, which was picked up by one of the boatmen.

Occurring fifteen years ago, it is yet fresh in the minds of the people of Del Norte. On winter evenings, around the family hearth-stone or in public places of resort, when other subjects have been exhausted, the wreck of the Brother Jonathan is brought up again, and the story, with all its horrible details, is discussed with subdued voices by the older members of the circle, and listened to with deep interest by the younger ones. Nor is this the only way in which the memory of the sad affair is kept alive. In the cemetery at Crescent City, a number of grassy mounds, with a decaying slab at the head of each, bearing the inscription:

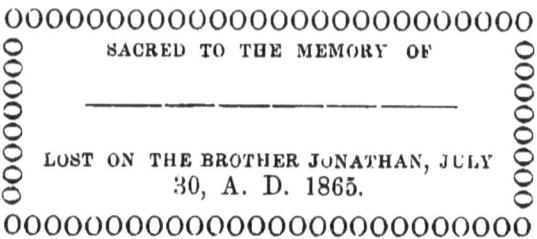

SACRED TO THE MEMORY OF

LOST ON THE BROTHER JONATHAN, JULY 30, A. D. 1865.

serve as a perpetual reminder of the Brother Jonathan disaster, and testify to the weakness of man as compared with the power of nature.

The years between 1865 and the present time (January 1st, 1881) have passed away with but little of interest occurring, and the remainder of this history, down to January 1st, 1881, will necessarily be disconnected and meagre. Such incidents and facts as have been deemed worthy of notice will be found in the succeeding pages of this chapter.

A high tide in 1866 did considerable damage to property at Crescent City. Several buildings were washed away by the tide, including a part of a large brick warehouse belonging to W. A. Hamilton, a warehouse belonging to Dugan & Wall, and Marhoffer's brewery.

On Thursday, September 12th, 1872, the first number of the Crescent City Courier appeared. It was published and edited by Walter B. Thorp. Its editor was young and energetic, and the Courier was well gotten up and presented a neat appearance. Several years had elapsed since the publication of the Crescent City Herald, and since that time the town and county had been on the down grade.

At last, however, the lumber trade was started here, and from that time on a steady improvement in the condition of the county was noticeable. There were no exciting, feverish speculations in town lots and mines as in days of old, but the trade of the county was based on a surer foundation. The farmers throughout the county were cultivating more land every succeeding year, and but little produce was being imported.

Chrome was discovered about twenty miles north east of Crescent City, on the Low Divide, and chrome ore soon became a prominent article of export. The copper mines, which had been discovered several years before, were idle, and the capital with which to work them to advantage was not forthcoming.

Some of the ladies and gentlemen of Crescent City organized a literary society in December, 1872, having for its object the mutual improvement of its members, and the passing pleasantly away of the long winter evenings. It is mentioned here by way of contrast with the present condition of things in Crescent City. Then, the community were public spirited enough to provide a place of profitable resort at least one evening in the week. Now, they are content to see the boys and young men of the place frequent the saloons (having no other place in which to seek amusement,) and are apparently blind to the advantages which a reading room and literary society would give the rising generation.

The monotony of Crescent City life was somewhat disturbed in the beginning of the year 1873, by the attempts made to enforce the provisions of the new Codes in relation to keeping open places of business on Sunday. It had been generally understood that on the first of January some of the officials would try to enforce these provisions, and a petition had been circulated and signed by fifteen or twenty citizens, asking that they should be enforced. The first Sunday in January came on the 5th, and it is supposed that the officers of the law were for once on the look-out for offenders, for on the following Monday morning a complaint was filed against David E. Shipman, for "a violation of the Sunday law by keeping his saloon open for the purpose of transacting business on that day." Mr. Shipman pleaded guilty, and had the pleasure of paying the fees of the District Attorney, Justice of the Peace and Sheriff. The next person engaged in the "unholy traffic" arraigned before the bar of justice was Peter Darby, Esq., who endeavored to convince the zealous limbs of the law of the error of their ways, by standing a trial. It was then discovered that the new Codes had not been received, and in view of that fact, the Attorney for the People went on with the prosecution under the old law of 1861. Mr. Darby was found guilty of a violation of that law, and he too was compelled to contribute his mite in the shape of fees to the District Attorney, Justice and Sheriff. Mr. Smith, who kept a saloon in the City Hotel, was the next in turn. Whether he was a descendant of the celebrated John Smith is not known; but it cannot be denied that his unassuming modesty and honest truthfulness appeal strongly to our admiration. He was taken before the Justice, and stated that "he had only sold one drink, in the morning, and that he had forgotten (?) that it was Sunday." In view of this frank confession, Mr. Smith was "let off easy"---by paying the regular fees. The next and last victim was John Riebert, who stood a trial, and was found guilty. This gentleman shared the fate of the member of the Smith family, and more too; for he refused to comply with the request to empty thirty-one dollars into the official pockets, and was therefore taken into the charge of the Sheriff and lodged in jail. After remaining in the county jail about twenty-four hours, he was released upon his friends paying the legal fees.

Considerable excitement was created by these proceedings, and some indignation was expressed in regard to the manner in which they had been conducted.

The "Old Guard" and their doings had long been a standing joke with the Crescentonians, and they were not surprised on receiving a notice that on Sunday, January 19th, 1872, there would be a meeting on Battery Point for the purpose of devising some means to amuse the citizens on that day. The public were not informed who would be the orators of the day, but it was stated that it would be attended by those who were not on intimate terms with the Sunday law. On the following week a card was published, purporting to come from "J. S. DeVoe, President of the Old Guards," as follows:

"In accordance with custom, the Old Guard think it proper to publish the results of their 64th anniversary, which took place on Battery Point on Sunday last.

Pursuant to call, on Sunday morning at eleven o'clock, the Guard repaired in full force to the Point, where they becomingly commemorated the times of yore. The Guard take this method of thanking all for their presence and hearty co-operation.

Financially, the affair was a grand success, as the proceeds over and above all expenses amounted to 6 cents, which sum is now on deposit with the undersigned, as a relief fund for the county officers, (with three honorable exceptions----Clerk, Treasurer, and Coroner,) who are requested to call and receive the same. If, however, they fail to make their appearance within ten days, said six cents, or such portion as is not then called for, will be turned over to the school fund of the county. J. S. DeVoe, President."

In accordance with a published notice calling a meeting of the citizens of Crescent City for the purpose of choosing judges and clerks of an election to be held on the afternoon of the first of March, to get an expression of the public sentiment as to the enforcement of the Sunday law, a number congregated at the Court House on Saturday evening, February 27, and chose the following officers of election: Judges, Franklin Johns, Edgar Mason and Jas. Harper; Clerks, Wm. Saville and J. E. Marhoffer. The result of the election was an overwhelming vote against the enforcement of the law. Of the 76 votes cast, 70 were found to be in the negative, 3 in the affirmative, and 3 scattering. Of course, the only effect this election could have was to reflect the sentiments of the community in regard to the law. But this little breeze in the quietness of Crescent City life soon subsided, and things resumed the even tenor of their way.

General Ray, a gentleman from Carson, Nevada, arrived at Crescent City in July, 1872, for the purpose of inspecting the beach mines some four miles below the town. He pronounced them the best he had ever seen for gold, platinum and magnetic iron, and he expressed himself well satisfied that they would return large profits to any party undertaking to work them with the modern improvements. The mines were then worked under the old process of mining, viz: wheel-barrow, tom, and sluice, and consequently a large amount of the mineral went to waste. Several of these mines were lying dormant for want of capital and suitable machinery to work them. The fact of the richness of the beach mines, and the opportunity presented for the profitable investment of capital, were more than once brought to the notice of parties who were ready and willing to engage in the development of the mines; but for ten years past Crescent City has been noted for the "freezing out" process, by which all who will not accede to the exorbitant demands of a certain class are met with such opposition, and so many obstacles are placed in their way, that it is impossible to invest capital with profit to themselves. The enterprise and sagacity that characterized the Crescent City merchants in early

days has long since passed away, and many of the most
enterprising of her early residents are either dead, or have
moved to other lands. The few who remain have lost the
vim and pluck of their younger days, and have fallen into
a deplorable " don't care " condition, neither beneficial to
themselves or the county. This is the plain, unvarnished
truth, and it will do no good to disguise it. And it is not
surprising that when a certain party, having a knowledge
of the modern methods of mining, and supplied with improved machinery, proposed to work the beach mines extensively, he should meet with oppositon. The party arrived on a steamer having on board the necessary machinery for working the mines, but learning that the part
of the beach he proposed to work had been "jumped" in
his absence, and that an exorbitant price would be demanded for it, he did not remove the machinery from the
vessel, and returned to San Francisco, leaving the would-
be speculators in mining claims to mourn their loss.

Nor is this tendency to drive enterprising men to the
wall confined to mining. In many other ways is the enterprise of the town demonstrated to be of the wrong
sort. True, there are always to be found men who are
willing to do all in their power to help along any project
for the material development of the town and county.
But there are not wanting as many more who meet the
enterprise with their opposition, and crush it out of existence.

A few minutes before nine o'clock on the evening of the
22d of November, 1873, the people of Del Norte county
experienced the heaviest shock of earthquake that had
ever occurred within their recollection. As near as could
be ascertained the vibrations were from South to North,
and continued nearly thirty seconds. The shock was so
great that it caused the fire bell and City Hotel bell to
ring, and houses bounced around as though they were
mere jumping jacks. All who found themselves able to

move rushed into the street in the wildest state of mind, expecting every instant that their houses would fall to the ground, and that a tidal wave would sweep them into eternity.

The damage to property in Crescent City was estimated at $3,000, and it was fortunate that so little damage was sustained.

It is said that fully one-half the chimneys in town were more or less injured, and that the cost of repairing them amounted to about $250.

In Smith's River Valley considerable damage was done, nearly all the chimneys being shaken down. The shock seemed to be the most violent on the sand hills, as large cracks from six to eight inches wide were reported in several places.

At Happy Camp the shock lasted about twenty-five seconds, and the rumbling noise accompanying it appeared to sound as if it was running nearly North and South. The wooden buildings rocked to and fro, and the tin pails hung up in Camp & Co.'s store swung backwards and forwards at an angle of nearly 45 degrees with the ceiling. Very little damage was done, however, except to the nervous system of the inhabitants.

The shock was felt more or less severely at other places in the county; in fact, curiosity regarding earthquakes had been fully satisfied, and people had reason ever after to be averse to visitations of the kind.

The spring of 1874 saw the usually quiet town of Crescent City in a blaze of excitement, for it was thought that silver mines of the richest kind had been struck, and that a new Comstock would be located in Del Norte county. The ore was found in the Myrtle Creek Mining District, situated about twelve miles in a north-easterly direction from Crescent City. The first discovery of the mineral is alleged to have been made in 1871 by a man named Blalock, who sunk a shaft and satisfied himself of the genuine character of the rock. He then covered up his developments, and for some reason or other kept the matter to himself, neither making any effort to work the mine himself, or inform anyone of the quality of his prospect. The fact of this discovery was kept a profound secret for over three years, when in some way the matter leaked out, and the consequence was the excitement above referred to. The excitement in Crescent City was attended by the usual scenes of a mining craze. Groups of men on the street were exhibiting to each other the results of the numerous tests of the rock which had been made, some saying that they could find no silver, while others asserted that it was $300 rock. A new mining district was formed and the whole country in the vicinity of the first discovery taken up. But this excitement, like many another in Del. Norte, soon subsided without any move being taken to develope the newly discovered mines. The locators were convinced that it required money to work quartz mines, and they knew that they did not possess it. And instead of making an effort to induce capitalists to give the project of opening the mines their attention, they resumed the usual routine of village life. The fact that silver bearing rock had been found in Myrtle Creek District was believed by all; but because of this neglect to bring the matter before men who were able and willing to invest in mining enterprises, the excitement was soon numbered with the things "that were."

Mr. Gus. DeYoung, one of the DeYoung brothers who have of late years brought themselves into public notice as publishers of the San Francisco Chronicle, paid Del Norte a visit in the summer of 1874. He was then publishing the "Commercial Directory of the Pacific Coast," and his visit was for the purpose of acquiring information for a Directory of Del Norte county. It was represented that the Directory would contain "information of general interest pertaining to the commercial and industrial interests of the county, a description of its general features, and many other desirable matters of general interest." Whether Mr. DeYoung interviewed the "oldest inhabitant" in his search for information, or whether he was deficient in geographical knowledge, is matter of conjecture; but the certainty that the good people of Del Norte were considerably surprised when they read the information in regard to this county, is not open to doubt. For the "Directory of Del Norte county" located Crescent City on the wrong side of the bay on which it is situated, and informed the people of Smith's River that their little village was located on Table Bluff, Humboldt county. In consequence of these blunders, the blessings that were showered upon his head were innumerable, and that word descriptive of the front part of a mill pond was many times prefixed to his name. Perhaps the inaccuracy and absurdity of the thing would not have been so universally noticed, had it not been for the known enterprise and intelligence of the DeYoungs.

The Valedictory of the Crescent City Courier, which had been purchased by Mason & Tack from Walter B. Thorpe, and published by them for a period of one year, appeared in the issue of March 13th, 1875. The publishers had probably found it up-hill work publishing a country newspaper, and had thought it the better part of valor to retire from the lists. The Courier did not remain long in its coffin. It was resurrected in November, 1875, by Silas White, its present publisher and proprietor.

From that time to the present, January 1st, 1881, nothing worthy of notice here has transpired. Trade has remained about the same for the last five years, during which time it has not been very active or large. Many improvements have been made in different parts of the county, noticeably in Smith's River Valley, where several fine buildings have been erected. Crescent City and Happy Camp have also improved of late years, and a disposition has been shown to rebuild old and decaying houses. In closing this chapter we bring this history down to the 1st of January, 1881. It has been endeavored to present such incidents, occurrences and information in the history of Del Norte as would be of general interest. Hoping that it may prove more instructive, and equally as interesting, we will now turn our attention to the scenery, climate, inhabitants, towns and villages, business houses and industries, commerce and trade, and the agricultural, mining and lumbering resources of Del Norte county----all of which will be described in as fair a light and with as much accuracy as possible.

CHAPTER V.

THE SCENERY, CLIMATE, AND INHABITANTS OF DEL NORTE COUNTY.

SCENERY.

The scenery of the Pacific Coast has always been a prolific theme for the pen of the writer, and the pencil of the artist has endeavored to transfer to canvass the beautiful landscapes, mountain views, and ocean scenes that meet the eye of the traveler in California. Its boundless plains, its snow-capped mountains, its fertile valleys and vine-clad hills, have inspired the admiration of the sightseer, the Muse of the poet and the genius of the painter. The famous falls and peaks of the Yosemite challenge the admiration of the world; the big trees of Calaveras are famous the world over. And they would be still more renowned, their beauties would have a wider and a greater celebrity, were it not for the fact that just such scenes are to be met with in a hundred different places in California. The counterpart of Yosemite, though on a smaller scale, may be seen in many places in the mountain ranges, and the trees of the Calaveras grove find rivals innumerable in the forests of the Northern Coast.

Many and varied as are the scenes to be met with in California, they are nearly all represented in the little county of Del Norte. Here may be seen smiling fields and lovely valleys, overshadowed by majestic mountains. Here the forests form a dark and massive background to valley, sea and town.

Standing on Battery Point, on a summer afternoon, the scene is beautiful in the extreme. Seaward, the setting sun casts a lurid glare over the waters, and seems to be going down in a blazing mass of fire; to the left and right the ocean meets the view, perhaps dotted by a solitary sail on the rim of the horizon, and with a long, trailing column of smoke marking the course of an ocean steamer.

To the south, following the line of the coast, the first objects apt to catch the eye are the red, glittering cliffs of Gold Bluff, in Humboldt county. Nearer, the rocks that mark the mouth of the Klamath River stand out in bold relief to the cliffs beyond. To the north, Point St. George, looking low and flat, juts out into the sea, with two or three tall, huge rocks, rising like sentinels on either side. Inshore, extending from Point St. George back to the top of the foot-hills, is an immense forest of giant trees, their rich green contrasting strongly with the high, barren mountains beyond, the peaks of the Bald Hills appearing clear and cold against the Eastern sky. Commencing at Battery Point, the crescent shaped beach extends six miles down the coast, its smooth, hard surface affording an excellent drive at low tide. A wharf extends out into the bay for the distance of a quarter of a mile, at which vessels are taking on cargoes of lumber. Directly opposite Battery Point, the Crescent City light-house, situated on an island about one hundred yards from shore, presents a pretty picture. It is a low, light-colored structure, facing the bay; from its center rises a tower, in which at eventide a revolving light guides vessels entering the harbor, and warns mariners at sea of the dangers of the rocky coast. A short distance south of the light-house, two large round rocks keep watch and ward over the bay, and to the south-east of the anchorage, Whale Island, containing about ten acres, a part of which is covered with grass, rises from the water to the height of a hundred feet or more. Crescent City mars the effect of the picture somewhat, appearing from Battery Point more like a collection of huts than a good-sized town.

Notwithstanding this slight defect, the whole scene is worthy of the pen of a Muir or the pencil of a Rembrandt. And it has always been a matter of surprise to me that the prominent painters of the coast, who visit the gorges and forests of Russian River, climb the steep sides of St. Helena, and see and appreciate the beauties of the Columbia River and the grandeur of Mts. Hood and Shasta, should pass Del Norte by without notice. Perhaps its remoteness and inaccessibility has had something to do with this; but I believe that a want of knowledge of the county has been a greater cause for its neglect by those who, if possessed of a better knowledge of its attractiveness, would not be slow in finding it out.

There are also many beautiful scenes in Smith's River Valley and vicinity. The little village of Del Norte is situated in the center of the valley, and in proportion to its size is better built than any other place in the county. Its white houses contrast pleasantly with the green fields and forests, and the scene is one of a quiet, peaceful nature. Walled in on two sides by the high mountains of the Coast Range, which here reach their highest altitude and wildest character, and shut off from the outside world on the other sides by the forest and the ocean, the sense of isolation is so strongly felt and so oppressive, that it can never be shaken off by a person once used to the busy life of thickly settled communities and commercial centers. But while the scene is fresh, and the place new to one, the beautiful scenery claims the admiration it deserves, and holds the eye of the stranger with fascinating power.

Other places in the county possess as beautiful, if not more beautiful scenery, especially the Low Divide. A wagon road leads from the valley up the mountain to the mines on the Divide, eight or ten miles from Del Norte. From the summit the eye takes in a vast number of ravines and gulches, while the fantastic shapes of the rocks and cliffs indicate that they were thrown up by some great convulsion of nature, ages ago, when the world was young. And if the sense of isolation in the valley is oppressive and powerful, the feeling of desolation and loneliness with which the view here impresses one is greater and more powerful still. All around, on every hand, the mountains are bare and bleak, while the solid, mighty upheavals of rocky heights are seamed all over with the defacing marks left by the war of the elements, and at the same time in their enduring grandeur seem to mock the ravages of time. Precipices, almost perpendicular for a thousand feet or more, make the head dizzy in viewing their great depths. At the bottom of the ravines, trees which from the top appear but tiny sapplings, are in reality several feet in circumference.

At Altaville, the scene reminds one of the lead mines in Missouri or Iowa. When copper and chrome was first discovered at Altaville and the mines worked, the little town was full of life and activity. Now it is deserted, and but few of the buildings remain. Black mouths of tunnels appear in the hill-sides, and heaps of blueish colored rock show the locality of the mines; shafts and mounds of dirt indicate the place where the prospector expended his time and muscle, and numerous ravines and hill-sides bear witness to the fact that prospecting was once extensively carried on here.

Once seen, Altaville clings tenaciously to the memory. It haunts one like a dream; the grand scenery of the surrounding country leaves an impression on the mind which time will not efface; and if the scene, with the indescribable quietness and peacefulness which give it its chief charm, could be represented on the canvass of some of our great painters, no doubt it would create an excitement in the world of art; no doubt artists and lovers of art would turn their attention to this long neglected region, and the tourist's tent form an object in many a landscape.

At Happy Camp, the scene has been thus described: "The town is beautifully situated upon a large and level flat. On the south, the Klamath River, with its immense volume of water, sweeps past it in bouyant waves and with a strong current, and on the west, cutting the town in twain, the gurgling and babbling waters of Indian Creek flow, and mingle with those of the Klamath, in plain view of the town. Its natural attractions and its salubrious climate are not surpassed anywhere. In the spring and early summer, especially, owing to the luxuriance of vegetation and the delicious coloring of the pine-clad hills that surround the place, every scene in the landscape looks so bewilderingly beautiful that no pen can portray all its beauties, no one approach a just realization of the many points of interest spread out on every hand."

And Happy Camp has seen times when the natural beauty of the place was intensified by the myriad fires of the savage blazing from every hill-top, the lurid glare from which lit up the surrounding mountains, and caused them to assume a fearful and wierd beauty; when the dark recesses of the mountain gorges grew black and hideous as a background to the gleaming flames; when the Indians, resplendent in paint and feathers, flitted like phantoms between the fires and the darkness beyond, chanting their war songs and stirring the signal lights to flash up brighter and brighter, sending their mysterious meaning far over the country, filling the hearts of the whites with fear.

But that was long ago, and is now well-nigh forgotten. Peace and good order reign supreme, and it can be truthfully said that no prettier picture can be found in California than this little mining town, set like a gem in the midst of the mountains.

On the various forks of Indian Creek are some magnificent scenes. The South Fork is the largest and most turbulent, and its scenery the wildest and most picturesque. The sources of this water-course are on the storm-worn sides of Mount Poston, a lofty, barren peak in the Siskiyou Range, rising 10,000 feet above the ocean. The Happy Camp correspondent of the Crescent City Courier in 1873, thus describes the scenery on the South Fork of Indian Creek:

" Here Nature has piled up a heterogeneous mass of mountains, covering their bases with dense forests, and their sides and crests with granite rock, leaving their accumulating waters to their own devices to find an outlet. This the waters of the South Fork have done by tearing down the shoulder of a mountain here, wearing away the adamantine sides of another there, forming vast gorges, whose deep recesses and snow-covered sides a vertical sun only could light up, and chasms whose depths were appalling----dashing, leaping, and foaming through their self-made rocky bed, until they are caught by the daring hand of man, and by judicious damming their wild turbulence toned down and made to do duty in converting trees into lumber. Again seized upon by the meddling hand of man, they are conducted to a receptacle that winds its serpentine course, like a monstrous reptile, on the face of the mountains, now winding its course through the dense growth of the primitive forest, now on the edge of a frowning precipice, and anon it stalks with its spider-like legs through intervening chasms, until the once leaping waters come in sight of the swift rolling, far-journeying Klamath, when they are again harnessed to do duty in extracting the precious metal from the gravel flats oper-

ated upon by the Happy Camp Hydraulic Mining Co.,
and then are allowed to escape,

'Flowing on and on forever,
To the sea or parent river '"

CLIMATE.

The climate of that portion of the county near the seacoast, comprising Crescent City and vicinity, Elk Valley, and Smith's River Valley and vicinity, is in its general character very mild and healthy. Severe frosts are seldom experienced, the heat in summer is not oppressive, and although little or no rain falls during the summer months, the close proximity of the ocean lends moisture enough to the atmosphere to sustain the vigorous growth of plants. The temperature is nearly the same throughout the year, there being but little difference between the winter and summer months. During five months of the year, from the first of November to the first of April, rain falls almost incessantly, and occasionally furious wind storms occur. The rain falls not the same every year, some seasons passing away with comparatively little rain, while others are remarkable for a heavy rain fall. There is very little and sometimes no rain during the summer months, the only disagreeable feature being the blustering winds which often sweep the coast. These winds are from the north-west, and often increase to furious gales, felt most disagreeably by the inhabitants. Smith's River Valley is somewhat protected by mountains on the north and north-west, and therefore the force of this wind is broken, and it does not make itself so disagreeably felt there. Indeed, it is doubtful if the whole Pacific Coast can offer a more delightful climate during the summer months than Smith's River Valley.

Happy Camp is situated ninety miles east of Crescent City, in the Siskiyou mountains. The warm gulf-stream of the ocean, which has such a great influence on the climate of the rest of the county, has little effect on that of Happy Camp, and during the winter season it is sometimes very cold there, snow frequently falling to a considerable depth. The surrounding mountains are covered with snow during a greater part of the winter, and the trail between Crescent City and Happy Camp is sometimes covered to the depth of fifteen or twenty feet. During the summer months it is much warmer than at Crescent City, the heat of summer being more intense than the cold of winter.

Having thus given a brief description of the scenery and climate of the county, we will now notice the

INHABITANTS,

Who hail from all parts of the Union and from various foreign countries, besides the native population, known as Digger Indians.

Del Norte county has a population of 2,669, including Indians and Chinese. The last census shows that on the first day of June, 1880, there were within the Twenty-fourth Enumeral District of the Third Supervisor's District of California, comprising Crescent, Smith's River and Mountain Districts, 1,980 inhabitants. Of this number 214 were Indians, 179 Chinese and 2 Negroes. In addition to the above, there were residing in the so-called Klamath Reservation 82 Indians. Of this number 32 were bucks and 30 squaws over ten years of age, and 9 bucks and 11 squaws under ten years of age. The report of the Census Marshal states that said Indians live by hunting, fishing and working for the whites. In the District comprising Happy Camp there were 597 inhabitants, 57 of whom were Indians, 230 Chinese and 5 Negroes. Total, 2,669.

The voting population is 697, and an examination of the Great Register discloses the fact that they came from East and West, from North and South; from the forests of Maine, from the tropical clime of the South, from the Northern and Middle and Western states; and from the far-off lands of England, Australia, Nova Scotia, France, Germany, Switzerland, Norway and Sweden. Other countries are also represented, and Del Norte may claim as cosmopolitan a character as any county in the State.

Of the voters of foreign birth Ireland furnishes 51; England and her possessions, includiug Wales, Canada and Nova Scotia, 57; Germany, including Prussia, Bavaria and Baden, 49; France, 5; Russia, 2; Australia, 2; Chili, 4; Scotland, 6; Switzerland, 5; Austria, 4; Sweden, 8; Denmark, 5; Norway, 3; Mexico, 1; Spain, 1. Among the occupations, farmers and miners take the lead, there being 127 of each. Next come loggers, numbering about 75; next, carpenters, of whom there are 30, including cabinet makers. There are 25 dairymen, and other occupations are well represented.

The white population, as a class, are well-to-do, but unfortunately for themselves are not overburdened with that spirit of enterprise which has contributed so largely to the prosperity of other portions of the State. Morals are no worse, and perhaps better, than in other counties in the State. A criminal act is of rare occurrence, and the Courts have but little business to attend to.

Of the Chinese population it is not necessary to say much. We of the Pacific Coast are too well acquainted with their vile habits, their thieving ways, and their contaminating influence, to render a description of the same either interesting or profitable. There are in this county about three hundred natives of the Flowery Kingdom, a majority of whom are engaged in mining. The principal part of these are at and near Happy Camp. Crescent City has a Chinese population of between fifty and one hundred. It is difficult to estimate the Chinese population correctly, because crowded as they are into filthy dens, there is no means of estimating their number by the number of houses they inhabit, and since the last census their number may have been augmented or decreased without any perceptible change in the appearance of Chinatown. As in every town in which they congregate, they have sought the most central part of Crescent City; and on the principal streets of the town their sign-boards point the way to wash-houses or dens of iniquity. As a general rule their shanties are surrounded by mud, filth and garbage of every kind---fit surroundings for such a degraded class. And to crown all, the perfumes----not of Arabia, but of Chinatown----the 1001 different and distinct smells of Chinatown, rise up in one grand, overpowering stench. And to their discredit be it said, those people of Crescent City who are the loudest in their denunciations of the Chinese are the very ones to give them employment. While crying down the evil of Chinese immigration, they lend it their aid by employing Chinese.

There are seven Negroes in the county, but one of whom resides at Crescent City. He is named after a celebrated poet, Byron, and in politics is a " black Republican."

The native population, the Digger Indians, are worthy of a more extended description. Their numbers are few, and they are rapidly diminishing under the hand of disease and death. And whatever their ancestors may have been, it is certain that Cooper's ideal is not to be found among these Indians at the present time. But there are many evidences that their former life, in comparison with that of to-day, was freer, happier, and more independent. Like all unlettered people, they have handed their history down in traditions, more or less superstitious, and tinged with that belief in Good and Evil Spirits which has always found a place in savage minds. These traditions point directly to the fact that years ago, before the white man set his foot on their hunting grounds, the Indians inhabiting the Northern coast were brave in war, fearless in the chase, independent, and possibly more intelligent than at the present time.

And it is an interesting fact that contact with the whites has served to sink them deeper and deeper into the mire of sloth, ignorance and superstition. Their present life is the most abject, the most degraded, that it is possible to conceive. Living in filthy huts, they keep from starvation by catching and drying salmon in the fall, and by killing sea-lions A few of them also occasionally work a day or two for the whites. Sometimes a dead whale comes ashore on the beach, when the Indians come from far and near and cut it up and carry it to their villages.

Their are several Indian villages in the county, the principal one being situated near Crescent City. To one not familiar with their ways, a visit to their village is full of interest. The writer in company with several others, visited the Indian village at Crescent City during the progress of a "ten night's dance."

We were carefully picking our way among the collection of huts and mounds, toward the one in which the dance was being held, when our attention was attracted by loud and monotonous sounds issuing from a hut on our left. We turned aside and approached this hut, where, we were told, a "war-dance" was being conducted. Looking in through the open door, (for unlike the majority of their cabins, this had a plank floor and a good sized doorway,) we saw a score or more of Diggers, of both sexes, fantastically decked with feathers and bedizened with paint. After the momentary lull caused by our presence, the Indians joined hands and formed a ring, and commenced a queer kind of a hopping dance, at the same time uttering a course, guttural sound, interspersed with hideous yells. Presently, a big buck, gay in feathers and bright paint, darted into the ring, dancing from side to side, keeping time to the monotonous music, and then darted out again. In a few minutes the same performance was gone through with again, and we were informed that this was kept up the whole night, without any change or variation.

Proceeding to the hut in which the "ten night's dance" was being held, we found that it, like most of the others in the village, was built after the true Digger style. An excavation had been made, somewhat similar to a cellar, and around the sides of this excavation had been placed on end boards and plank, the dirt being thrown up against them on the outside. Other plank had served to make a roof, and a hole had been left in the middle of this to allow the smoke to escape. In one end a small aperture did duty as a door.

Stooping and entering through this hole in the wall, we found ourselves in the midst of a curious scene. Around a fire in the center of the dirt floor, was a motley collection of Indians and white spectators. At one side of the room a long pole stretched from one end to the other. Behind this pole was a kind of platform or shelf, built close to the wall; and on this shelf was something which looked, in the indistinct light, so like a coffin, that an involuntary shudder crept over one. It seems that when a female of this tribe reaches the age of puberty, a ten-night's dance is held to invoke the blessings of the Great Spirit upon her future life. And in this box, which at first glance we took to be a coffin, we were informed the object of the ceremonies lay. With joined hands, forming a line in front of this box, outside the pole, with their backs to the fire, stood forty or fifty Indians, of both sexes. They were bare to the waist, and stood as motionless as statues. Suddenly a big buck at the head of the line uttered a low, humming sound, and instantly the whole line took up the note, at the same time slowly swaying with one accord from one end of the room to the other. The monotonous sound increased in volume, growing faster and faster as it grew in sound, the swaying bodies keeping time in their vibrating motion, until it reached its greatest height, when it slowly descended so low that it could scarcely be heard. Then the whole performance is gone through with again, and this is kept up for ten nights in succession, without intermission or variation. On the morning of the eleventh day the Indians form in rings of eight or ten, with one in the center, and in this manner dance round and round until they reach the seashore, where they plunge into the surf, cleansing themselves of sin and dirt at one and the same operation.

Were it not for the unbearable fishy smell which pervades the hut, one might stay for hours watching the curious scene. And it would require a better pen than mine to describe it as it deserves-- the monotonous chant of the dancers; the long, swaying line keeping time to the rude music; the smoke from the fire lazily ascending toward the aperture in the roof; the group of spectators; the fire, fed by some savage hand, now flashing up brightly, disclosing as if by a calcium light the bare backs of the dancing Indians, the earthen walls, and the shelf before which the dancers stand -- now dying slowly out, transforming the swaying bodies into ghostly forms, and peopleing the shadowy corners with dusky shapes of evil; bringing visions of Dante's "Inferno" vividly to the mind, and impelling a glance toward the doorway, half expecting to see. inscribed above it. "Abandon hope, all ye who enter here."

The other principal Indian rancherias in the county are situated at Happy Camp and Smith's River. There is also an Indian rancheria on the Yontocket slough, which empties into Smith's River about a mile below the village.

The chief characteristics of all these Indians are filth, superstition, ignorance and degradation. There are a few exceptions as regards intelligence, but even the most intelligent among them do not rise above the level of the lowest of the whites. One of the Crescent City Indians, the Indian Doctor, seems to be a sort of second Denis

Kearney, so easily does he dupe his followers. Whether this particular M. D. resorts to politics, medicine, or religion to pull the wool over the eyes of his people, I know not; but I am inclined to think that he is a sort of Priest among them, with power to cast out devils, forgive sins, and by incantations and magical ceremonies "cure all the ills that flesh is heir to."

Perhaps the Doctor has borrowed some of his cunning from his brethren of the Catholic Priesthood, for he evidently makes free use of that most powerful factor in the Catholic religion----superstition. He is fond of promenading the streets of Crescent City with a string of little bells jingling from his clothing, and a bone through his nose. His face is like parchment, and his whole appearance is that of an animated mummy. His eyes have a shrewd, cunning expression, and he is possessed of more intelligence than a majority of his tribe.

The customs of the Del Norte Indians are full of interest, and if space permitted, a long account might be given of their manner of living and traits of character. They have a code of laws independent of the laws of the whites, which has probably been handed down from generation to generation from time immemorial. The gist of their law is, that one who does an injury to another shall suffer to a like extent, and that money shall be the panacea to smooth all wounded feelings, and compensate for all wrongs less than murder. If an Indian kills another, whether right or wrong, according to their established custom, his life must pay the forfeit. If he wrongs another, no matter how trivial the offence, he must make amends to the sufferer by a liberal donation of "a la-ka-chick," the medium of trade among the Indians.

From the fact that this Indian money has been used by them as long as the whites have had any knowledge of them, we may infer that when they were strong in numbers and divided up into many tribes, a considerable trade must have been carried on between them. Money sprung from the necessity of commercial nations to possess a convenient representative of value, to facilitate trade and business exchange between different countries; and as the representative of property, it has existed among all people and in many various forms. The Indian money is a kind of shell, obtained from the ocean, and it is said to be almost as hard to find as the white man's gold.

The Indians of this county have acquired but few of the virtues of the whites and many of their vices. They drink whiskey whenever they can get it, they will gamble away the clothes from their backs, and they are not excessively honest. They take a deep interest in the 4th of July and election day. In fact, the Smith's River Indians have endeavored to imitate the whites by electing a Chief, Lieutenant and Captain. The elections are held in Brooking's Hall, Del Norte, and are conducted in the following manner: Squire Brooking sits at his desk, a small box at his right, a cup filled with black beans, white beans and buttons at his left. The Indians are seated on the benches in front of the Squire. Three candidates for Chief announce themselves. Then Squire Brooking explains to them that the white bean stands for one (naming him) the black bean for another, and the button for the other. The Indians then walk up to the stand and each place a bean or a button into the box, and when all have voted the result is ascertained by counting the number cast for each candidate. The defeated candidates look almost as blue as their pale-face brethren who run for office and go up "Salt River," and their successful opponents are apparently in high spirits.

The estimated number of Indians in the county is 270, besides 82 on the so-called Klamath Reservation.

A few years to come will see the last of these Indians, who once roamed the forests and mountains of Del Norte in large numbers, and who could then truly boast that they were "monarchs of all they surveyed." Flying before the march of civilization like chaff before the wind, they have rapidly been reduced in numbers, until at the present time, a mere remnant of the earlier tribes are left to go down with the setting sun of their declining strength.

CHAPTER VI.

TOWNS AND BUSINESS HOUSES OF DEL NORTE COUNTY.

The following description of the towns and business houses of the county has been prepared with a view to accuracy rather than for effect. It has been said that "to overestimate a thing is worse than to underrate it." Fully impressed with the truth of this saying, I will not attempt to give a false coloring to the condition of the county or the enterprise of its business men. If the present condition of the county is not what it should be, if its trade languishes on account of the narrow-minded views of its merchants, it would be folly to cover up the fact by an account of enterprise which does not exist. The first and most important place in the county is the county seat, the town of

CRESCENT CITY.

The tract of country in which Crescent City is situated is somewhat remarkable by its location immediately at the foot of the Coast Range of mountains, which elsewhere, from San Francisco to Columbia River, with few exceptions rise abruptly from the Pacific Ocean without leaving more of low bench land than here and there a sandy beach, or the bottom grounds of a river that finds an outlet in the sea. On the right-hand, running due north with the

Humboldt meridian, is the Redwood ridge, from three to six hundred feet high, forming the first bank or tier of the Coast Range, which, after passing Smith's River, turn to the left to close up again with the ocean.

That part of the plain, thus singularly isolated between the mountains and the sea, on which Crescent City is situated, is thus described by N. Scholfield, a surveyor and geologist, who passed along the coast in 1854, and whose observations were afterwards published:

"Crescent City is situated on the southerly side of a low promontory extending from the great Coast Range; the extremity of this promontory forms Point St. George, and consists of table land, elevated some fifty or sixty feet above the surface of the ocean. This table is underlaid by igneous unstratified rock, which appears mostly in boulders, as shown by the bluffs where they have been denuded by the disintegrating action of the sea, and by boulders composing a reef extending outward. On the north side, this promontory consists of low sands, and in the interior is a shallow laguna of considerable size. The southerly side, at the site of the town, consists of low timber land, scarcely elevated above the possible reach of running tides."

The harbor of Crescent City affords good shelter in summer, when the wind generally blows from the northwest; but it is open and unprotected against the southerly gales which prevail during the winter months on this coast, and which at times cause a heavy swell to set in from the south-west, dangerous to vessels in the harbor. It is conceded by all that this danger might be obviated by closing up with a breakwater the gap, half a mile wide, between the headland of Crescent City (Battery Point) and the rocks south of it. Vessels can find good anchorage in five or six fathoms of water, and if needed improvements to the harbor were made it would be safe at all seasons of the year. The harbor has no bar, being an open roadstead. It is situated 280 miles north of San Francisco, about midway between it and the Columbia River. Resolutions have repeatedly been introduced in Congress for building a breakwater here, but have resulted in nothing more than to cause the harbor to be surveyed two or three times by the Government.

Perhaps the best evidence of the dangerous character of the harbor during the winter months, and the necessity for improvements, could be furnished by the Underwriters, who lose large sums every winter on account of vessels that part their lines and go ashore on the beach at Crescent City. The smooth character of the beach saves vessels going ashore there from becoming total wrecks, but the heavy surf pounds them against the ground until they sustain severe damage, costing large sums to repair. Scarcely a winter passes away without seeing one or more vessels on the beach here, and this of itself should be enough to call for the aid of the Government.

Although it is estimated that it would require $3,000,000 to build a complete breakwater here, a much less sum, say $500,000, would suffice to make such improvements as would render the harbor safe at all times.

Crescent City, as seen from the ocean, does not present a very attractive appearance. The buildings are nearly all low, one story, or one story and a half, and as seen from the deck of an approaching steamer, the town looks like a collection of huts. The place improves on a nearer view, and perhaps it is the grandeur of the surrounding scenery which gives it such a dwarfed, poor appearance at first sight.

It is well laid out and compactly built. The buildings are nearly all of wood, superior lumber being manufactured here for building purposes. Spruce and fir are mostly used for building, redwood not being suitable for that purpose. There are twelve brick buildings and one stone ware house.

Crescent City contains a population of about 1000, and the district polls a vote of 305.

There are two churches, one Catholic and one Methodist.

Several secret societies flourish here, namely, the Odd Fellows, Freemasons, Good Templars and Ancient Order United Workingmen. The Masons have a fine hall, the largest building in town, and the order is in a prosperous condition. The Odd Fellows have a strong lodge, and the Good Templars are flourishing. The United Workingmen, but recently organized here, are rapidly increasing in numbers, and are likely to prove a strong and prosperous lodge.

The schools of Crescent City are among the best in the State, and at the Centennial Exhibition in 1876, Crescent City received credit for the best exhibit of work done in the schools of California. From the report of the public schools of Crescent City for the month ending December 22, 1880, by H H. Heath, Principal, it appears that the whole number of children enrolled in the school is 120, viz: Enrolled in Principal's room, 33; enrolled in 1st Assistant's room, 41; enrolled in 2d Assistant's room, 46; total, 120. The total number of children in the county, between five and seventeen years of age, entitled to school money, is 477. The amount of school money appropriated to Del Norte county in 1880 by the State School Superintendent was $629.64, giving to each child in the county $1.32.

Of the business houses of Crescent City, three are general merchandise stores, one groceries and provisions, one fancy goods, books and stationery, two stoves and tinware, one boots and shoes, one harness and saddleryware, one drugs and medicines, one bread and confectionery, and nine saloons. There are two barber shops, two tailor shops, one millinery shop, three shoemaker's shops, one cabinetmaker's shop, two watchmaker's shops and two blacksmith shops. There are two livery stables, and one feed store. There are three hotels, and one restaurant. The largest stores in Crescent City or in the county are those of Hobbs, Pomeroy & Co., and J. Wenger & Co. Both stores are in fire-proof brick buildings. In the rear of Hobbs, Pomeroy & Co.'s store is a large frame warehouse, with room for the storage of many tons of merchandise. The firm carry a ten thousand dollar stock of general merchandise, besides doing a general commission business. They have two other ware-houses, one stone and one brick, where goods to be forwarded by them to the interior are stored. The company also own the Elk River Mill and box factory, employing a large number of men in the manufacture of lumber and boxes. This alone is sufficient to give them a large trade, and together with their other business foots up many thousand dollars a year.

J. Wenger & Co. carry a four thousand dollar stock of general merchandise. This firm own the Lake Earl Mill.

The Crescent City Wharf and Lighter Company, Johnson & Malone, own the wharf at Crescent City. They have in connection with it commodious ware-houses on Front street, in which goods are stored till delivery. Owing to the rocky character of the ground in which the piles are driven and the heavy swell which strikes the wharf during the winter season, a portion of it has been several times carried away by the sea, and the owners have been put to great expense in repairing damages to the structure. The railroads of the Elk River and Lake Earl mills extend to the end of the wharf, where vessels load with lumber from the mills.

There are two newspapers published in the county, the Crescent City Courier, Silas White, editor and proprietor, and the Del Norte Record, J. E. Eldredge, proprietor. Mr. White, a stalwart Republican, publishes a neutral paper, and the Record, published by a strong Democrat,

is afraid to say so and supports no politics in particular.
The next place in the county worthy of mention is the
village of

DEL NORTE.

Nestled at the foot of the mountains, Del Norte, Smith's
River Valley, forms a pretty picture. The houses are
white and new-looking, and contrast pleasantly with the
surrounding forests and fields. There are about thirty
houses in the village, most of them being well built and
handsome. There is a neat little church in the village,
built by the Methodists. The public school is taught by
two teachers, usually having an attendance of about fifty
scholars.

There are in the place two general merchandise stores,
one hotel, two blacksmith shops, one harness shop, two
shoemaker's shops, one variety store, one cooper shop,
one grist mill and three saloons.

About four miles from Del Norte, near the mouth of the
river, a general merchandise store is kept by Mrs. Westbrook, and half a mile further on, at the mouth of Smith's
River, is situated the Occident and Orient Commercial
Company's fishery and cannery.

Before observing the operations of the workmen in the
cannery, we will note its situation and surroundings.
Smith's River, a clear, limpid stream, heading away off in
the Siskiyou Mountains, the snowy summits of the lofty
peaks among which it takes its rise being visible from
Happy Camp and vicinity, empties into the ocean a short
distance below the cannery. Near its mouth are a number of sloughs, branching out from right and left, and
during the fishing season these waters are literally alive
with salmon. The fishing season extends from the first
of September to the middle of November. A smooth,
level beach affords excellent facilities for hauling seines,

and as the fishing is not interfered with by rapid currents or obstructing drifts, it is an easy matter to catch and handle the fish.

Let us now proceed to the beach near the mouth of the river and watch the seine gang at their work. There are from ten to fifteen men at this work, and their operations are conducted in the following manner: First, a large seine is taken out into the middle of the river in a boat, and another boat takes one end of this and moving in a semi-circle lands the end on the beach some distance down the river. The first boat then takes the other end to the shore, and the men prepare to haul the seine. The seine is made of heavy twine, the netting being too large to detain the very small fish, and too small to allow the large ones to escape. The net is gradually hauled in to the beach, and here and there inside the bobbing corks which uphold it, a leap, a flash of silver sides and a dash of spray, betray the efforts of a captive salmon to free itself from the confines of the net. Slowly it is hauled in by the strong arms of the men, and as the two ends converge and the semi-circle narrows and closes, the water is lashed into foam by the crowding numbers of the finny tribe. Large flat bottomed boats are rowed alongside, and when the seine is hauled in the fish are thrown into these boats. The fish caught weigh from five to sixty pounds. Loaded in the boats, the fish are taken to the cleaning room, a small building extending out some distance over the river. Here there is a chute which is lowered to the level of the boats by a rope and pulley worked by steam power. It is filled with fish and hauled up, when it empties itself on the floor of the cleaning room. Five or six men then cut and clean the fish, when they are taken to the cutting room. In this room they are placed upon a machine having six large knives, equal distances apart, and cutting pieces to the right lengths for cans. These lengths are then passed to a table where they are split up ready for the filling department. In the filling department about twenty men are employed in filling the cans. On each side of a long table the fillers are ranged, and after seeing the operation of can filling but few would have a taste for canned salmon. The men employed in this work at the Smith's River Cannery are nearly all Chinamen, and the disgusting manner in which they cram the pieces of fish into the cans with their claw-like fingers is enough to sicken any ordinary mortal. After being filled the cans are taken to the soldering machine. This little machine does more work in a day than twenty men would do in the ordinary way in the same time. A small furnace rests on the floor, and on top of this furnace is a groove filled with solder, kept hot by the fire in the furnace beneath. At the left of this furnace is an inclined plane, connecting with the groove, over which is a receptacle from which acid drops on the cans. At the right of the furnace four wires stretch from the grooves across the room, the third wire being lower than the others. The cans are first placed on the inclined plane, when they roll across the furnace, the bottom edge resting in the groove, passing through the hot solder on to the wires, from which they are taken and carried to the stoppers. The duty of the stoppers is to stop the vent-hole in the cans, which they do by the use of fire-pots and irons. There are fifteen men in the stopper's department, who daily stop the vent-holes in 10,000 cans. The cans are next taken to the testers, who put them in iron coolers, each holding 120 cans, which they lower by means of a pulley into a cooking kettle. This kettle holds five coolers, and is filled with water heated to a boiling point by steam-pipes leading from the boiler room. If the smallest possible hole happens to be in a can, the contents will fly out through it on being subjected to the action of the boiling water. After being tested the cans are again lowered into the cooking kettles, and allowed to remain five hours and a half, which is sufficient time to thoroughly cook them. When the cooking process has been gone through with, the cans are placed in a tank filled with lye, to take off the grease, after which they are dipped into a large tank of cold water, and then taken to the cooling room. When they are thoroughly cool they are ready for the process of lacquering. This consists in dipping the cans into a compound, half asphaltum varnish and half turpentine. This compound is known as Egyptian lacquer, and is used to prevent the cans from rusting. It gives them a light gold color. It requires fifteen or twenty minutes to dry the cans after this process, when they are ready for the final process of labeling. This is done by women and girls. A bright girl can label 2,000 cans in a day. In the casing room three men case up the cans, each case holding four dozen, and they are now ready for shipment.

There has been a fishery at the mouth of Smith's River for over twenty years, but the present extensive cannery was established only a few years ago, the fish having formerly been put up exclusively in barrels. In 1877, Wm. Fender, the owner of the property, leased it to the Occident and Orient Commercial Company, for a term of ten years. Since the above named company came into possession of the property they have expended nearly $8,000 in improvements. The main building is 200 feet long and 60 wide. The machinery in use in the cannery is of the best make, and everything is conducted in an economical, business like way which cannot fail to insure success.

The average catch of fish is from 100 to 1,000 at a haul, and as many as 1,500 have been caught at one haul of the seine. The capacity of the cannery is 10,000 cans per day. The number of hands employed during the fishing season is from 60 to 75, and the wages paid are from $1 to $2 a day.

During the season of 1880, 158,750 cans, or 7,000 cases, and 300 barrels were put up, which were worth in the

San Francisco market: Cases, $6 per case; barrels, $5 per barrel; making the value of the whole, $43,500.

Some difficulty is at present experienced in shipping the goods to San Francisco. The entrance to the river is dangerous for either sailing vessels or steamers, on account of sunken rocks in the channel. An appropriation of five or ten thousand dollars, applied to the improvement of the mouth of the river, would be sufficient to make a safe and easy entrance. And when the wise Solons who are sent to represent Northern California in Congress devote less of their time to making buncombe speeches and advocating measures as foreign to the interests of their constituents as China is to Maine, we may hope that something will be done for the improvement of the mouth of Smith's River.

If the needed improvements were made to the river, not only would the fish from the cannery be shipped, but lumber from mills on the river, minerals from the Low Divide and produce from valley farms would also form a portion of the exports.

There are only three villages of any importance in the county, the third being

HAPPY CAMP,

Situated ninety miles east of Crescent City. It is built on both sides of Indian Creek, near its junction with the Klamath River. Surrounded by mountains as it is, the only means of reaching it being by mountain trails, it yet has a thriving trade. The country around it is rich in mineral wealth, and a large capital is invested in mining property.

There are four stores at Happy Camp, three kept by white men and one by Chinese. They deal in general merchandise such as miners and farmers need. There are two hotels and two saloons. The stores do a large business, and it is said that they pay annually freight charges to the amount of twelve or thirteen thousand dollars in gold coin.

The above comprises all the business houses in the county, with the exception of a few cooper shops in Smith's River Valley. In the next chapter the lumber resources of the county will be considered, and the mills described.

CHAPTER VII.

THE LUMBER RESOURCES OF DEL NORTE COUNTY.

From the southern line of Del Norte county, extending to the dividing line between California and Oregon, is a vast forest of the finest timber in the world. This belt of timber reaches from the shore of the ocean from ten to twenty miles back into the interior. The variety is mostly redwood, spruce and fir, though some cedar is found at a distance from the coast. The trees are of immense size, many of them being from ten to fifteen or twenty feet in diameter. It is almost impossible to estimate the amount of this vast body of timber, or the wealth which it will yet bring to Del Norte. Already the manufacture of these giants of the forest into lumber is becoming the chief industry of the county, and in the near future Del Norte will export more redwood, spruce and fir than any county in the State. Other lumber counties in California are fast losing their forests and will soon have no lumber to ship. The lumber business here is just in its infancy. The lumber now sawed is but a trifling amount to what will be cut in a few years to come. Its future value to the county cannot be overestimated. The capital now lying useless in city banks will in a few years find a safe investment here. For it is certain that as the production in other parts of the State decreases, more attention will be directed to the forests of this county. A short time ago the San Francisco Bulletin, reviewing the lumber interests of the Pacific Coast, said:

"The redwood and sugar pine forests of California are of great value, and, in the near future, must rank among the three or four greatest resources of our State.

"California redwood is now laid down in Denver, Colorado, though the freight charges on the Union and Central Pacific railroads are $250 per car-load of ten tons. But clear redwood, costing $24 per thousand in San Francisco, still manages to compete on favorable terms with pine cut in Colorado gulches, and with white pine brought from Chicago.

"Indeed, it is only a question of a few years when the forests of the Pacific Coast will be taxed to their utmost resources to supply the demands made upon them. Those who purchase timber lands at the present time are wise in their generation. The forests seem wide, and even inexhaustible; but how much of the great forest belt along the Atlantic is left to-day? It is among the coming events that the tallest pines of Puget Sound shall fall; the deepest forests be pierced with the steam saw and engine, which are taking the place of axemen and loggers. Agriculture, mines and forests are the three pillars of the future, and the interests of the lumber trade appear likely to receive a mighty impetus within the next decade.

"A comparatively slight lowering of freight charges would enable Pacific Coast lumber to be laid down in Chicago at a profit, and thus inaugurate a business of constantly widening dimensions, giving employment to thousands of men, and building up cities in places now covered with thick forests."

The timber lands in Del Norte county that may easily be made available are estimated as follows: Elk Valley, 24,300 acres; Smith's River, 51,200; Mill Creek, 48,000; Klamath River, 115,200; making a total of 238,700 acres. This estimate includes only those sections of timber land that may easily be made available. Taking the low estimate of 250,000 feet of timber to the acre, the above area would represent a total of 59,675,000,000 feet.

Calculating the number of working days in saw-mills at 300 per annum, and limiting their capacity to 25,000 feet per day, these forests would furnish material: To one saw mill, for 8,525 years; to five saw-mills, for 1,705 years; to ten saw-mills, for 853 years; to twenty saw-mills, for 426 years.

The dimensions as well as the kind of timber growing in this section, preeminently fits the same for ship building purposes, and this industry will some day occupy an important position here.

There are at present five saw-mills in the county, with a capacity of 11,500,000 feet per annum.

The vast lumber resources of this county were left apparently unnoticed and absolutely unheeded until the year 1869, when a meeting of the citizens of Crescent City was called for the purpose of taking steps toward the manufacture of lumber. At this meeting a company was formed, having in view the building of a large steam sawmill, to cut lumber for exportation. Work was immediately commenced, and, chiefly through the unremitting personal energies of Jno. H. Chaplin and J. Wenger, Sr., within a few months a mill was completed. The mill is called the Lake Earl Mill, and is situated about three miles north of Crescent City, on a large Lagoon known as Lake Earl. The Lagoon is some ten or twelve feet deep, and is separated from the ocean by a narrow strip of sand beach, through which the water filters, and some say that the ebb and flow of the tides are perceptible on the lake. It frequently happens in winter, when the waters of the lake have accumulated to an unusual height by continued rains, that it breaks through the narrow barrier into the ocean; at which times it nearly empties itself and assumes the appearance of an extensive swamp. A slough once stretched from the Lagoon across the low timbered land to Smith's River, which leads to the supposition that at some former period the river emptied into the lake.

Owing to the fact that the Lagoon, as stated above, is liable in times of high water to break through its banks, leaving but a few inches of water, and rendering it impossible to float logs, the Lake Earl Mill has been forced to remain idle four or five months in the year. Many schemes were devised to remedy this draw-back. A flume and gates were built at the mouth of the Lagoon, but failed to stand the force of the floods. Then a ditch was dredged out in the lake through which to raft logs to the mill. This project was also abandoned, as the shifting mud and sand in the bottom of the lake soon filled the ditch up again. Last year a dam was built across the head of the lake, about a quarter of a mile below the mill, with gates so constructed that during the rainy season the surplus water can be let out. Inside this dam there is always sufficient water to float the largest logs. It will easily hold 3,500,000 feet, enough to keep the mill running nearly the whole year. The mill is connected with the Crescent City wharf by a railroad.

The capacity of the Lake Earl Mill is 32,000 feet per day. The lumber sawed is mostly spruce The mill runs double circular saws, besides edgers, slab saws, planers, etc. The circular saws are 64 and 60 inch. The men employed in the mill number 30; in logging camp, 30; total number of men employed, 60. The wages paid are from $26 to $75 per month and found.

From January 1st, 1880, to January 1st, 1881, the Lake Earl Miil sawed 4,000,000 feet of lumber, 500,000 feet of which was sawed for home consumption, and the remaining 3,500,000 feet shipped to San Francisco. The value of this lumber was $30,000.

J. Wenger, Sr., one of the owners, is Superintendent of the mill. It is thought that since the dam has been constructed across the head of the lake, thus insuring a sufficient quantity of logs to keep the mill running a greater part of the year, the annual product of the mill will be largely increased. Before the dam was built, it was impossible on account of low water to raft enough logs to the mill to keep it running. As it is now the logs can be rafted to the head of the lake during high water and secured inside the dam, from which they are drawn into the mill by steam power.

The largest mill in the county, and one of the finest on the Pacific Coast, is the Elk River Mill, at Crescent City. Winding down through a low, marshy prairie for several miles, is a small creek called Elk River, emptying into the ocean in the lower end of town. On this creek, a short distance above its mouth, the mill and connecting box factory are built.

The Elk River Mill was built in 1871, and is owned by the firm of Hobbs, Pomeroy & Co. The mill is two stories high, the upper story being occupied by the saw-mill, the lower story by the box factory; an engine-room on one side of the main building. Elk River, the creek beforementioned, brings the logs down from the woods, about three miles away. The creek is about five feet deep, and logs nine feet in diameter can be rafted to the mill, those larger than that being split in the woods. Arriving at the mill, the logs are hauled up an inclined plane by steam power, the whole work being controlled by one man. They are then given in charge of the head sawyer, who, by means of levers and pulleys, turns them onto the carriage at his pleasure. While being sawed the logs are moved on the carriage by screws, turned by one man. The mill runs triple circular saws, the first a 64-inch saw, the second a 60-inch, and the third a 50-inch saw; also, a 21-inch horizontal. There are also on the mill floor a 50-inch pony, one edger, one slab saw, two trimmers, one picket saw, one lathe saw and one planer. The planing machine is worthy of special notice. It can plane from 10-inch timber to a small moulding. Its capacity is as follows: Surfacing, from 15,000 to 18,000 feet per day; tongue and grooved, 13,000; rustic, 12,000.

H. A. Peeples is Superintendent of the mill. It has been under his supervision for about one year, and during his management many improvements have been made. The planing-room has been enlarged, and the large planer now in use was put in to replace two smaller ones. Mr. Peeples has had the new machine placed in a different position from the others, and the room for piling lumber designed to be run through the planer has been increased two thirds. Formerly, the lumber, after passing through the planer, was carried from the machine and run through a chute to the yard. This unnecessary work has been avoided by placing the new machine in such a position that the lumber may be run directly from it into the yard. Another improvement has been made in the manner of working up lumber into pickets. Formerly, the lumber being first sawed above, was then run through a chute down stairs, carried to a saw, and after being worked up into pickets carried out into the yard. The necessity for this unnecessary work has been obviated by placing on the upper floor a saw in such a position that no unnecessary carrying of timber is required, and the pickets are loaded on cars and run directly from the saw to the yard. Other improvements to the mill are contemplated, among them the replacing of the screws now used by steam head blocks. The present mode of turning screws is very heavy work, and but few men can do the work for any considerable time without losing health and strength. One man can easily handle the head-blocks, by means of a lever and steam power. It is also intended to replace the edger now in use with a Stearn's gang edger.

The capacity of the mill is from 45,000 to 50,000 feet per day. The greater part of the lumber sawed is spruce and redwood, only a small amount of fir being sawed, and that for home use.

The box factory occupies the lower floor of the building. The most of the boxes made are bread boxes, next sugar boxes, next boxes for canned goods, made for the packing house of Cutting & Co., San Francisco; also a large number of coffee and spice boxes. The box factory turns out from 1,500 to 2,000 boxes of all kinds per day, and its management requires a man who has been years in the business, and who understands every particular in regard to the box trade. Chas. W. Blake, the Superintendent, has occupied his present position for over four years, and is evidently the "right man in the right place."

It is interesting to watch the progress of the lumber from the time it is taken from the yard till it is put up ready for shipment to San Francisco as box material. The lumber used for boxes is mostly spruce, though a few redwood boxes are occasionally made. The lumber is first taken from the mill up stairs to the yard, where it is left to dry. From four to six weeks is sufficient for this purpose, and it is then loaded on cars and taken into the factory.

We will follow a car load as it is taken in by the men, and observe the various processes through which it passes. Just inside the door is a circular saw, called an edger, and the lumber is unloaded within a few feet of it. Then the sawyer places one end of a plank on the table of the saw, and pushing on the other end drives it across the table, where it is caught by his assistant and pulled through, the saw taking off an edging of any desired width. It is then passed on to the man at the planer, who runs it through the machine, after which it is taken to a cut-off saw and cut into right lengths for boxes. These lengths, an inch and a half thick, are then placed on trucks and wheeled to a self-feeding, re-splitting machine, and after being split by this machine are passed to the packers.

The packers press and tie into bundles called shooks the sides, tops and bottoms. The ends are nailed with light strips.

One million feet of lumber from the yard is yearly worked up in the factory into boxes. Besides this, 250,000 feet of slabs and waste lumber from the mill are annually worked up into sugar boxes and small bread boxes. This is all worked up while green, and is then piled in dryhouses and in the yard until dry, when it is put up in shooks like the others, ready for shipment.

The machines and saws in the box factory are: Three large splitting saws; one self-feeding re-splitting machine; two small saws for general use; two cut-off saws; one horizontal 42-inch header; two planers, one a double surface, and the other a single-surface; and one edger, also used for splitting.

The motive power of the mill is furnished by an engine, 20x24 inches. Another engine, 12x14, furnishes power to the box factory. There is also a very small engine for lathe work. Four tubular boilers furnish steam to these engines, and are each 54 inches in diameter, 16 feet long, with 50 3-inch tubes. A small boiler is to be added, for the purpose of supplying the lathe engine with steam.

The number of men employed is: In mill, 50; in box factory, 20; in logging camps, 30; total, 100. Wages, from $20 to $75.

From the 1st of January, 1880, to the 1st of January, 1881, the Elk River Mill sawed 6,000,000 feet of lumber, and the box factory worked up 1,250,000 feet into boxes. Value of lumber sawed, $60,000.

A iron track railroad, one mile in length, extends from the mill to the end of the Crescent City Wharf.

Hobbs, Pomeroy & Co. own 1,600 acres of available timber land. Nearly all the lumber cut by the Elk River Mill is shipped to Hobbs, Pomeroy & Co.'s box factory in San Francisco, the largest box factory on the Pacific

Coast. The lumber is there worked up into boxes to fill transient orders, the boxes made in the Crescent City factory being principally stock. Very little spruce from this mill is placed on the market as lumber, almost the whole of it being used in the manufacture of boxes.

As the box factory in San Francisco is connected with that at Crescent City and owned by the same company, a brief description of it will not be out of place here. It is situated on the block bounded by Beale, Market and Main streets. The building occupies nearly a whole block, being 300 feet long and 45 feet wide, and has entrances from Beale and Main streets. It is three stories in height. Upon the first floor the rough lumber is cut into suitable condition for box material, and it opens out into a large yard where an extensive supply and great variety of lumber is kept. This floor contains a steam engine, three planing machines and nine circular saws, besides other smaller machinery. In this department a large force of men are employed. If an order for a hundred cracker or shoe boxes is received, they could be put through the machinery on this floor in about two hours, and be ready for delivery an hour later.

An order for a lot of boxes first goes from the office to the foreman of this floor; he estimates the number of feet of lumber required to fill it; the order is then passed on to a man in the yard, who selects the lumber; thence with the lumber to two others, who edge off the boards; thence the boards go along to the planing machine, thence to three men who cut them into proper lengths with a circular saw; thence to the men who re-saw, or split them into thinner boards, by means of self feeding re splitting machines; thence they are piled upon the elevator and sent up to the second and third floors.

Upon these floors the parts of boxes are first placed, the ends by themselves, the sides also, and are then nailed together and stored away, or delivered to order from slides running out into Main or Beale streets. Ten or fifteen thousand boxes are kept constantly on hand. About 75 men are employed.

The nail bill of the establishment amounts to over $500 per month. Until quite recently boxes were nailed by men, a rapid nailer constructing 100 per day. But the inventive genius of the age has come to the aid of the box manufacturers, and they now have nailing machines, each of which do the work of six men.

The shooks sent down from the factory at Crescent City are put together by these machines. The box trade is constantly increasing, and probably in a few years will warrant the enlargement of both factories.

The Smith's River Mill is situated twelve miles from Crescent City, on the banks of Smith's River. It is run by water power and is capable of cutting 5,000 feet per day. All of the lumber cut by this mill finds a ready sale in home markets.

The Big Flat Mill, owned by the Big Flat Gold Mining Company, was built for the purpose of sawing lumber for use in the mine, and is situated on Growler Gulch, Big Flat. Logs are hauled down the gulch and up a skid road. The lumber is carried to the ditch by an endless wire-rope elevator, run by an undershot water wheel.

In addition to the above named mills, there are three small mills near Happy Camp which saw lumber for home consumption, each cutting about 5,000 feet per day.

We have had the Stone Age, the Bronze Age, and the Iron Age; and we have now entered upon the Wooden Age. And it is an interesting subject to calculate the length of time the forests will last at the rate they are being consumed at the present time. It has been asserted that it will be but a few years before the builders of the nineteenth century will be forced to find some other material for building purposes. This may be true of certain portions of the country, but it can hardly apply to Del

Norte. There is enough timber in this county to keep a dozen large mills at work for a thousand years. The only things necessary to make this the most important lumbering point on the Coast, are a good harbor, a liberal investment of capital, and more enterprise on the part of its citizens. The annual production of lumber in Del Norte county is at present about 11,500,000 feet, and there is no reason why it should not reach ten times that amount.

CHAPTER VIII.

THE MINERAL RESOURCES OF DEL NORTE COUNTY.

GOLD.

Gold mining in Del Norte county has been steadily and successfully pursued since 1851, and it is at present the most important of its industries. The placer diggings on Smith's River and on the Klamath, the black sand on the ocean beach, and, more especially, the extensive hydraulic mining carried on in the region of Happy Camp, all demonstrate everywhere in this section the presence of gold in paying quantities.

Happy Camp is the only section of the county that has yet received any benefit from capital. A large amount of money has been invested in Happy Camp mines, and they are now being worked on a profitable basis. Most of the mines there have been worked for years, and have always yielded a good return for labor and enterprise.

The most important mine in the Happy Camp District is that of the Del Norte Hydraulic Mining Company, S. S. Richardson, Superintendent. The diggings of this mine are situated a mile above Happy Camp, on a large flat. A ditch over ten miles long, and five feet wide at the bottom, conducts water from Elk Creek to the mining ground. This ditch has proved very expensive to the owners. Owing to the light and porous nature of the ground through which it passes, it requires continued "puddling" to keep it from leaking; and it frequently breaks down during the winter season. The outlay of capital in the Del Norte Hydraulic Mine has been about $50,000. A small saw-mill has been erected on the company's ground, for the purpose of sawing lumber for their own use. About 25 men are employed in this mine.

The Happy Camp Mine, Ferguson & Frazier, owners, is situated upon Chaney's Flat, a large flat that has an unbroken gold-bearing deposit of hundreds of acres. The owners have a full head of water, and employ 12 men, piping all the gravel, boulders, etc., through their sluices that the water will carry off. The company also own a small saw-mill.

The other important claims are the Wingate Hill Hydraulic Mine, owned by Temple and Childs, work 12 men; Bunker Hill Hydraulic Mine, owned by Temple & Childs, employ from 5 to 10 men; China Bank Hydraulic Mine, owned by J. K. Reeve, employs from 8 to 12 men----has a valuable saw-mill; Muck-a-muck Hydraulic Mine, works from 5 to 18 men. Besides these mines, there are various river bar claims, worked and owned principally by Chinamen.

There are several mines in the vicinity of Happy Camp now lying idle, which only need capital to make them paying properties. Near Happy Camp, and on Indian and Clear creeks, a million dollars might be profitably invested in mining. Point Lookout, an old mining locality, was several years ago worked with various success by many parties. Indian Flat, another old mining locality, is situated on the other side of the Klamath and almost directly opposite Point Lookout. Between it and Muck-a-muck Flat, a distance of six miles, is a continuous range of gold-bearing gravel deposits, extending at some points several miles back from the river. When capital shall be brought to bear upon these localities, rich returns are almost sure to follow.

Various places on the different forks of Indian Creek long since abandoned by those who had to depend upon their own strong arms to wrest the gold from the hard cement and adamantine rock, can be made to pay well by the use of improved machinery, and under the supervision of practical miners.

The gold mining districts comprising Big Flat, Haynes Flat and French Hill will prove to be the richest in the State, should they ever be properly developed. The Big Flat is the richest of these localities, and miners have worked there more or less since 1854. Owing to the difficulty of procuring water with which to work the vast gravel deposits of Big Flat, comparatively little gold has been taken out there of late years. In 1877 Harry Harvey, H. Mulkey and Captain Fauntleroy located claims there. Messrs. Mains and Hickock also had claims there.

In 1878 the Big Flat Gold Mining Company, commonly known as the Boston company, bought forty acres of ground from John Mains and worked during the first winter with the gulch water, and the following spring they commenced a ditch, seven miles long, from Hurdy Gurdy Creek. The ditch was soon completed to Growler Gulch, at which place they commenced mining during the month of March, 1880, at the same time continuing the ditch from that place to the ground bought from Mr. Mains. They used a No. 5 Giant, running about 1200 inches of water.

For a time all went swimmingly. The Big Flat Company's principal place of business was at San Francisco, but it also had an office in Crescent City. Work at the mine was apparently prosecuted with great vigor, and the community were confident that the Big Flat Gold Mining Company were rolling in wealth, and fortunate was the man who got a position in the mine. But observant people after a while noticed, that it required several clerks to sweep out the office and read the newspapers at Crescent City; that these same clerks seemed to have little to do and plenty of time to do it in; that they spent most of their leisure time (about 23 hours out of the 24) in buggy riding, pool playing, and other pleasant but costly diversions----all this indicating that their official business was either very small, or that it weighed lightly indeed upon their high-toned shoulders. Visitors to Big Flat also insinuated that, like " our friends, the Bermudians," the Big Flat Company had one "boss" to every laborer. The rumors and suspicions thus set afloat were confirmed when pay-day rolled around and the men were informed that there was no money in the treasury to pay them for their labor. Work was discontinued at the mine, and a settlement was effected with the men by which they received 75 per cent. of their wages. But this was not the end. The affairs of the company grew from bad to worse, and finally the whole property, not excepting even the office furniture, was attached by several indignant creditors, who slowly awoke to the fact that they had been "sold again."

Of the present condition of the concern----whether the mine will be abandoned to the creditors, or whether more money will be advanced by the Boston share-holders---- but little is known. Certainly it is the opinion of a majority of the practical miners of the county that a well-directed expenditure of capital at Big Flat would open up a rich mining district, and yield large returns on the investment. But to accomplish such a result, there must be more laborers than officers; labor and capital must be applied to the best advantage. About $100,000 have already been expended at Big Flat, and an outlay of a few thousands more would put the mine in good working condition.

The Mountaineer Mine, near the Big Flat, is supposed to be very rich ground. It is intended to complete a ditch, part of which has been dug, from Jones' Creek to the mine The ditch will be five miles in length.

The Haynes Flat Mine is owned by a Boston and San

Francisco company. Work was commenced on Haynes Flat in 1877. About three miles of ditch and flume were built, but through a failure on the part of the company to advance the "needful," the work was discontinued and has not since been resumed.

The French Hill Mine has been worked to some extent for fifteen or twenty years. It is owned by a San Francisco company. Like the Big Flat Mine, it has met with financial difficulties, and the property was recently attached by creditors. It is understood, however, that an arrangement has been made whereby the debts of the company will be paid and work resumed.

There are other placers on Smith's River, which have been worked for years, and at times have yielded large amounts of gold.

Besides these gold deposits, there are several well-defined leads of gold-bearing quartz, and the black sands on the ocean beach are heavy with fine gold.

W. B. Mason and Jos. Connor own a gold-bearing quartz ledge on Myrtle Creek, and other flattering prospects of the same nature have been found.

The Bald Hill Quartz Mine is situated in the Bald Hills, about twelve miles north-east of Crescent City. It has been worked more or less for twenty years, but the parties prospecting it having limited means did not give it a fair test. Some very rich specimens have been found in spurs of this ledge. The Del Norte Gold Mining Company own the mine. The shares of the company are all held by gentlemen of Crescent City.

The beach mines are worthy of a more extended notice, for they are destined to form an important feature in the future interests of Del Norte, when the inventive genius of Edison or some other great mind discovers a method of separating the gold from the sand. The existence of vast deposits of gold bearing sands on the sea coast of California, Oregon and Washington Territory has been a matter of notoriety for a quarter of a century. The wealth of these deposits is fabulous. In 1852 there was great excitement in this State about Gold Beach or Humbug Mountain, in Southern Oregon, between Rogue River and Port Orford. The supplies for these mines were nearly all procured from the wholesale houses of Crescent City, and many accounts were given of the richness of these mines. In fact, so great was the rush of miners to this new locality, that it was feared the placer mines of this part of the State would become depopulated.

The largest deposits of gold-bearing or black sands are in the vicinity of Humboldt Bay, Gold Bluff, Klamath River and Crescent City. At Gold Bluff miners have been working for twenty years. The Gold Bluff mine is now the most extensively worked beach mine on the coast, the Gold Beach mine having been abandoned years ago.

In 1850, when this portion of the coast line was still in undisturbed possession of the Indian tribes, a party of adventurers traveled from Trinidad up, seeking for the mouth of the Trinity River, which, instead of being in reality an affluent of the Klamath, was supposed to have a separate mouth. One of the party was J. K. Johnson, now a resident of Crescent City. At a favorable spot on the beach they saw glittering particles of sand, and on examination found them to be gold. Gathering some of this gold, they went back to Trinidad, to procure provisions. On their return, however, they found nothing but a bed of gravel, a change in the direction of the surf having carried away or covered up the glittering treasure. After this discovery ensued the so-called "Gold Bluff excitement." The first mining claim was taken up the same year by Bertrand & Nordbamer. The sands were worked with sluices, the gold being caught in riffles sawed in a plank, loaded with quicksilver. From that time to the present the Gold Bluff beaches have been steadily worked, the highest amount taken out in any one year being $25,000 for the lower claim, about one mile below the upper bluffs.

One claim on the beach four miles from Crescent City has also been worked for several years. The return per ton of sand is very meagre, and the tailings prove by a careful assay to be nearly as rich in the precious metal as before washing. Attempts have been made to separate the gold from the sand by various processes with machinery, and by chlorination and boiling, until finally nearly all parties working these mines have returned to the old process of sluicing. Only a moity of the gold is obtained by this process, but the work pays a profit. The value of these sands is greatly increased by the quantities of platinum they contain, which is now wasted, owing to the imperfect manner in which the gold is obtained. The various processes hitherto tried have been unable to accomplish anything more than by the process of sluicing, and the beach mines of Del Norte will continue to expose temptingly before us their riches, until some inventive Yankee discovers a process for extracting the gold from the sand

The opinion has been held by some that this beach gold comes from the bottom of the ocean, but a majority believe that the gold comes from the bluffs along the coast, and that the action of the sea working night and day is the great natural separator. And it has been remarked that when the direction of the wind is such that the surf breaks square on the beach, it rolls up quantities of course gravel, and no black sand is visible; but that, when it cuts the beach at an angle, the gravel is washed into heaps in certain spots, and in others black sand is deposited, more or less rich in gold.

From a paper read before the California Academy of Science, Jan. 5, 1874, by A. W. Chase, the following in regard to this subject is taken:

"Many ideas have been advanced as to the probability

of gold in quantities, and course in character being found beyond the lines of surf, predicated on the fact that it in conjunction with black sand has been said to have been brought up from the bottom by the leads of sailing vessels, and I believe an expedition was fitted out to obtain the sand by means of a diving bell or some such apparatus, which did not result favorably.

"Two or three facts can be taken in consideration here to form an idea on this subject. The first is that the gold evidently comes from the bluffs. This no one can doubt after once viewing them. The second, that after "caves" the gold obtained is much coarser in character. The third, that it is only after a continued succession of swells that cut the beach at an angle that the rich sands are found. When the surf breaks square on, let storms be ever so heavy, it simply loads the beach with gravel. The fourth, that no one witnessing the power of the surf can doubt that it must have an immense grinding force. From these facts, I am inclined to believe that the gold follows the first two or three lines of breakers, and will never be found in paying quantities beyond."

The black sand is very heavy, but the gold obtained from it is so light that when dry it will float on the surface of water. Besides gold, the black sand contains many other varieties of minerals. Prof. Silliman, in his "Notes on the Mineralogy of California, Utah and Nevada," mentions a great variety of minerals as composing the black sands of Butte county, California. It is probable that all or nearly all of these will be found in the black sand of the ocean beach. As there are large deposits of chrome iron in Del Norte county, it is probable that chromite forms a portion of the black sand of this county. Prof Silliman mentions syenite as the matrix from which most of the minerals he enumerates came, and Mr. Chase, in the paper above quoted, states that it is a common factor in the gravel here. On microscopic examination, besides the gold and magnetic iron ore, the sand will be seen to contain minute and brilliant red particles, and other translucent particles will be seen. Prof. J. D. Dana, to whom a specimen of the sands were sent, says: "The red grains in the sand are ganet. It is probable that the deposit of sands dates partly from the close of the Glacial era; that is, the time of melting of the ice in the early part of the Champlain period, when floods and gravel depositions were the order of the day; and partly from the latter part of the Champlain period, when the floods were but partially abated, yet the depositions were more quiet."

SILVER.

There are several ledges of silver-bearing quartz in the county. In fact, nearly all the gold-bearing quartz contains some silver, and the copper and chrome ores contain more less silver. Time will demonstrate that there are silver mines here unequalled elsewhere on the coast.

COPPER.

The copper leads and beds in this county are well-defined and extensive. Copper ore was discovered in 1860 in the north-western part of the county, on the Low Divide. When these mines were discovered there was a great excitement and rush for claims, everybody ignoring the rule that it requires money to successfully operate in copper mining.

There are five good copper mines in the Low Divide District, viz: the "Hanscom," "Occidental," "Alta," "Union" and "Monmouth," all located on fine leads.

From 1860 to 1863 there was shipped from the "Alta" and "Union" mines about 2,000 tons of good copper ore, containing a large percentage of gold and silver. Owing to the high price of labor and transportation at that time,

the mines did not pay to work, the price of copper also
being very low. Wages for miners were from $75 to $100
per month and board; freight from the mines to Crescent
City, $10 per ton; lighterage, $2.50; freight to San Francisco, $10; drayage and wharfage in San Francisco, $1;
making on account of transportation from the mines to
San Francisco, $23.50 per ton.

At this present writing all this has changed. Wages
for miners are about $40 per month and board; freight
per ton, $6; freight to San Francisco, and wharfage, $4;
making the cost of transportation $10. The ore is very
rich, its market value per ton in San Francisco being $50
or $60. Fifteen thousand tons of copper might annually
be exported from these mines. For several years past
they have remained idle, the owners lacking the necessary
means or the enterprise to work them.

The Condon Copper Mine, at Big Flat, is the only copper mine in the county that has recently been worked to
any extent. It is supposed to be the richest copper ledge
in the State. Mr. Condon, the owner, has sunk a shaft
about 40 feet deep and 50 feet back in the hill. The ledge
is from 15 to 20 feet wide, and grows wider as it goes
down. While the shaft was being sunk a cave was broken
into in the middle of the ledge which was about 15 feet
square, and was on all sides rich with decomposed ore,
leaving what remained almost pure copper.

CHROME.

The chrome mines of Del Norte county are situated on
Low Divide Hill, in Low Divide District, and in the vicinity of the copper mines. Attention was first directed to
the chrome ores in 1868; claims were located, opened,
and worked in 1869. The Tyson Smelting Company, of
Baltimore, Md., shipped annually from 1869 to 1873, 1,500
tons of this ore. The total expense per ton, inclusive of

shipment to Baltimore, amounts to about $21. The ore averages 40 per cent. From 1873 to the present time the shipments have been irregular and light, and but little work has been done in the mines, the amount annually taken out averaging about 600 tons.

IRON.

The Low Divide District is one vast body of mineral wealth. Not only does it contain enormous quantities of copper and chrome, but immense deposits of iron ore, of various grades and classes, are found there. Iron ore is found in various parts of the county, but the bulk of it is situated in the Low Divide District, where the chrome iron mine of the Tyson company is situated. These iron ores have been tested by scientific men, who have all pronounced them as of very high grade. Besides the chromic there are deposits of the red and brown hematite, and the magnetic iron ores. Notwithstanding the fact that this vast mineral wealth lies at their very doors, waiting to be brought to the surface, the people of Del Norte do not seek to enlist the aid of capitalists to open the mines and build furnaces; indeed, the outside world is in almost total ignorance of the existence of these ores in Del Norte county; all owing to the lack of enterprise and business tact on the part of the business men of the county. Peradventure, if the Seven Sleepers were in the mining region of Del Norte, they would never be woke up by its "enterprising" citizens.

From the best information I have been able to obtain, it appears that but one attempt has ever been made to attract the attention of iron manufacturers to this locality. In the spring of 1874 Mr. Wm. Sublette, of San Francisco, spent two months prospecting with the view to ascertain the real extent of these iron deposits, and the facilities which exist for their profitable working. Mr. Sublette returned to San Francisco thoroughly satisfied that the deposits are inexhaustible, and that they can be worked cheaper, and, consequently with more profit than in any other locality on the Pacific Coast. He believed that these resources are bound to make Del Norte county the greatest iron producing section in the West. As the result of his investigations he announced that he found iron of all the various grades in abundance, with plenty of limestone necessary for fluxing purposes. Ample water power can be obtained on Smith's River, and the timber for charcoal is limitless. The iron ores are situated within twelve miles of Crescent City, which would be the shipping point. Mr. Sublette estimated that a company working on its own capital could lay down a tram-way from their furnaces to tide water at Crescent City, and deliver the pig iron there at a cost of about one dollar per ton. Transportation from Crescent City to San Francisco would cost about $3 per ton, making the entire cost of transportation only $4 per ton. Sydney coal, for blasting purposes, can be laid down at Crescent City for $7 or $8 per ton, by the cargo. Mr. Sublette endeavored to secure the necessary capital to work these mines, but failed to do so, and nothing has since been done in the matter. The value of these mineral deposits cannot be overestimated. From the time the first furnace was erected, a new era of prosperity would dawn for Del Norte.

COAL

Was discovered several years ago on Point St. George, and a company was formed to work the same. But like every other mining company, with the exception of the Tyson company, who have worked mines in the vicinity of Crescent City, the coal company was destitute of capital; and after sinking a shaft some seventy or eighty feet, and finding excellent prospects, they were compelled to suspend work at the urgent request of creditors. This is the only coal mine that has ever been worked here, though the same coal----a brown coal of valuable properties ---has been discovered in various parts of this section.

CHAPTER IX.

THE AGRICULTURAL RESOURCES OF DEL NORTE COUNTY.

That portion of the.Crescent City Plain comprising Elk Valley and Smith's River Valley consists of about 18 square miles of the richest and best agricultural lands, viz: Smith's River Valley, 15 square miles; Elk Valley, 3 square miles. The quality of the land varies somewhat in different localities, but in general it is a heavy, black soil, raising the finest of vegetables, oats, wheat and barley, and the best and most nutritious grass.

A comparatively small amount of the arable land of the county is cultivated, dairying being the great industry which requires nearly all the land for grazing purposes. Owing to this fact the amount of grain raised in the county is very small, not sufficient for home consumption. The yield of grain is about 30 bushels of wheat to the acre, 50 bushels of oats, 40 bushels of barley. Potatoes could be raised with great profit if the demand of the home market was sufficient to afford buyers for them. New land yields from 8 to 12 tons to the acre; land which has been under cultivation for years, from 2 to 5 tons to the acre.

There is a small amount of arable land in the vicinity of Happy Camp and on Indian Creek. The farmers there nearly all raise large quantities of vegetables, which find a ready sale among the miners at fair prices.

Fruit abounds in Del Norte county. A brief notice of

some of the fruits indigeneous to the Northern coast, and which may all be found in this county, is here given.

The thimbleberry is a small, luscious red berry, with a delicious flavor. They grow on a thornless bush, four or five feet high.

The salmonberry is of two colors, red, and dark yellow, and the bush is covered with spines or thorns, like the blackberry. The shoot continues to grow from year to year, and in time sheds its spines. The bush is sometimes three inches through near the ground, and ten or twelve feet high. The fruit is somewhat larger than the largest specimens of the Lawton blackberry, and they are the first fruit to ripen, commencing during the latter part of May and continuing till the latter part of June. The fruit is used in its raw state, fresh from the bushes, with cream and sugar. It has a plain acid taste, is not juicy like the thimbleberry and blackberry, and is not good for pies.

There are two varieties of huckleberries. The blue huckleberry is the finest flavored of all the native berries, of this region. Grows about two feet high; fruit ripens through July and August. Another species grows in the redwood forests eight to ten feet high; has a pleasant acid taste; ripens through summer to autumn.

The strawberry is found in small quantities on the sand ridges bordering the ocean, and on the warmest spots on prairies. Berry small, and of little account.

The blackberry is abundant. Any quantity can be gathered in close proximity to Crescent City.

Of the cultivated fruits, the apple and plum do exceedingly well. The apple lacks the rich flavor of the Oregon apple, but the plum is perfection itself. Apples keep all winter to April, and will stay on the trees until Christmas. Most varieties of pears do well. The raspberry and currant are perfectly at home, and some very fine varieties of strawberries are raised in Smith's River Valley. Some varieties of gooseberries do very well.

Besides the varieties of wild berries mentioned, there are several kinds of beautiful flowering shrubs, growing on the prairies and in the forests of the foot-hills. One is known as the Shrub Honeysuckle, growing on prairies, from four to five feet high. It bears a profusion of sweet scented flowers, filling the air with their delicate perfume.

In the forests of the foot-hills are rhododendrons and laurels with large, showy flowers, and other trees and shrubs worthy of a place in every garden.

The dairying interests are so intimately connected with the agricultural interests of the county, that they will be considered under the same head. The largest dairies are in Smith's River Valley. The following is a list of the principal dairymen and the number of cows milked by each during the season of 1880:

J. R. Nickel. 87; Wm. Robinson, 40; Mrs. Ann Rigg, 190; L. W. Jones, 53; Bailey Brothers, 55; J. H. Hall, 42; A. Grow, 7; F. W. Oberschmidt, 7; S. T. Youmans, 99; Theodore White, 51; Strain Brothers, 108; Henry Alexander, 33; D. R. Griffin, 30; Jas. Ewing, 18; Eli Howland, 40; Jos. Younker, 20; J. McLaughlin, 125; J. D. Kirkham, 9; H. C. Ransom, 180; H. Westbrook, 200; C. Woodruff, 11; C. Beam, 18; Jas. Hight, 10; Henry Marsh, 10; Denis Tryon, 200; Jas. Aulpaugh, 40; M. V. Jones, 70; L. DeMartin, 68; E. W. Smith, 110; J. Bertch, 39; Chris. Steiger, 15; J. Maris, 56; F. Gay, 25; F. Chapman, 25; others milking from 2 to 6 cows, making the total, 2,150 cows.

These 2,150 cows will average 150 pounds of butter to the cow, making the annual product of butter in Del Norte county, 322,500. Reckoning that this butter will net 25 cents per pound, which is a very low estimate, it will amount to the sum of $80,625. The Del Norte butter is of the very best quality, and is eagerly sought after in the San Francisco market, where it competes successfully with fancy brands from Marin and Sonoma counties. Every year the production increases, and in a few years it will probably reach a half million of pounds.

Before we take leave of the subject of the agricultural resources of the county, we will glance at the history, present condition, and agricultural, lumber and mineral resources of the Klamath Indian Reservation, in this county. In this Klamath Reservation, locked up by the Government, and rendered useless by the idiotic measures of the Indian Department, are thousands of acres of as fine timber land as the sun ever shone upon. And immense resources in minerals lie useless and idle because of the unjust and absurd policy of the Federal Government. A territory twenty miles long and two miles wide is kept sacred to the use of 82 Digger Indians.

When the Reservation was first formed in 1855, it was a necessity arising from the danger to be apprehended from three or four thousand Indians who were running over the county, threatening the whites, and making themselves generally obnoxious. This necessity has long since passed away. The Indians on the Reservation have decreased from over 2,000 to less than 100; and as most of their warriors and braves sleep in the embrace of death, there no longer remains any reason to fear them.

The Indian Department, entirely ignorant of the true state of affairs, or else careless and indifferent in regard to the matter, have turned a deaf ear to every appeal made to them on behalf of the whites. Our Congressmen have more than once been reminded that it was their duty to interest themselves in procuring an abandonment of the reserve by the Government, but have as yet accomplished nothing more than to make a repetition of the representations which have from time to time been made to the Indian Department.

Uncle Sam is a rich old gentleman. He is rich enough to give all who apply a farm, and he is as generous as he is rich. It is his evident intention that every man shall have a home of his own; for that purpose he has established land offices in nearly every section of the country. Laws have been enacted for the purpose of distributing lands among the people, and all the land laws seem to point in one direction, that is, that each citizen may acquire 160 acres of land. And if we admit that 160 acres of land are sufficient for a white man, who tills the soil and improves his possessions, then it is a matter of surprise that such an unjust discrimination in favor of the Indian as is shown by the Government regarding the Klamath Reservation should be made. There are about twenty-five able bodied male Indians on this reservation. A moments calculation, taking into consideration that the reservation is twenty miles long and two miles wide, will prove that each one of these Indians is allowed eight or ten times as much as a white man. And the injustice of the thing will be more apparent, if possible, by considering that the Indians occupying the reservation are of the lowest class of the slothful, ignorant Digger tribe, and that they are never known to bring an acre of land into cultivation, much less open mines, and convert timber into lumber.

It may be said in answer to this, that the amount of arable land in the Klamath Reservation is so small that it would not support any considerable number of settlers. Admitting this fact, yet it cannot be denied that there are lumber resources within the bounds of the reservation sufficient to give thousands of men employment; that the mineral wealth stored in its gulches and mountains would prove almost inexhaustible; that the salmon fisheries which would be established on the Klamath River would be another source of wealth and industry. By constructing a rock wall eight hundred feet long from the main land to a rock outside, the entrance to the river could be made safe at all times. Light-draft steamboats could navigate the river for 65 miles, from its mouth to Orleans

Bar, if a few thousand dollars were spent in improvements to the river.

All these facts show conclusively the reason for urging the Government to remove the Indians now on the reserve to some other reservation, and open the Klamath Reservation to settlement by the whites. The Indians could be easily removed to the Hoopa Reservation, about 50 miles above the mouth of the Klamath.

It was at one time believed that the reservation would be opened, and in this belief a number of settlers located on the reservation and made improvements to the amount of $10,000 or more. They continued in uninterrupted possession of their claims for over a year. M. V. Jones, of Crescent City, established a fishery at the mouth of the river, a tavern for the accommodation of travelers was erected by M. G. Tucker, and a ferry was also kept by the same gentleman.. There were located at the mouth of the river and vicinity a dozen settlers, and many others were preparing to locate there as soon as the Indians were removed and the reservation declared open Those who had already located felt that they were secure in their possessions. A postoffice was created by the Government and M. G. Tucker appointed Postmaster. This fact confirmed the settlers in their belief that the reservation was soon to be declared abandoned for Indian purposes. And great was their consternation when in the fall of 1877 they received an official order commanding them to vacate the premises immediately. The Legislature was then in session, and Mr. Tucker wrote to Jas. E. Murphy, Representative from Del Norte, requesting him to endeavor to procure a stay of proceedings and an extension of time in which to remove their property from the reservation. Mr. Murphy accordingly went to Gen. McDowel, Commanding the Pacific Coast Division, G. A. R., and laid before him the situation of the settlers and their request. As a result of this interview, orders were given that the time in which the settlers must remove from the reservation be extended six months. Six months passed and the settlers did not remove. Thus matters stood until July, 1879, when a detachment of U. S. soldiers ejected the settlers from the reservation.

So unjust was this proceeding considered, and so confident were the people that the Indian Department were in ignorance of the true state of affairs, that the aid of our representative in Congress was demanded, and a bill was introduced by Congressman Berry looking to the opening of the reservation to settlement by the whites. But Mr. Berry was probably too much engaged in other business to attend to the interests of his constituents, for nothing was accomplished by him beyond the introduction of the bill above referred to.

About the same time Bill No. 5038 was introduced in the House of Representatives by the Committee on Indian Affairs.

In April, 1880, a letter was received by a gentleman of Crescent City from Congressman Berry, reviewing the provisions of the bill above mentioned. The following is an extract from the letter alluded to:

"I think it (the bill) is wholly impracticable and will result in no benefit to the Indians, but be an absolute injury to them, and an injustice to every section of country in which a reservation is located. In the Klamath Reservation, the operation of the bill would be, if carried out, to tie it up for fifteen or twenty years; at least that is my judgment."

Representative Berry professed to take a great interest in the matter of opening the reservation to settlement by the whites, but this interest was manifested only in words, for notwithstanding a bill, No. 3454, was reported back to the House of Representatives by the Committee on Indian Affairs, to whom it had been referred, recommending in the most unqualified terms that it be passed, nothing more was done in regard to it, and up to the present time the matter remains in the same situation as before; indeed, our own Congressmen were so negligent that after the bill was reported back favorably by the Committee on Indian Affairs. no attempt was made to pass it through the House.

The Report of the Committee on Indian Affairs, to whom was referred the bill for the restoration of the Klamath Reservation to the public domain, is so full of information on this subject, that it is given here, without any apology for its length or the length of time which has elapsed since its return to the House:

House of Representatives,
May 7th, 1880.

[REPORT TO ACCOMPANY BILL H. R. 3454.]

"It is in evidence that the reservation in question was set apart for Indian purposes by executive order of Nov. 16, 1855, in pursuance of the act of March 3, 1855, relating to the Indians of California, and included the lands embraced in a strip one mile wide on both sides of the river for a distance of twenty miles from its mouth.

"The formation of this reservation was exceedingly wrong and unjust to the public interests, as it rendered all the lands lying outside, opposite, and adjoining the same comparatively valueless, as the water front on both banks was within the reservation, and the evidence discloses the fact that these adjoining lands are very valuable for the timber growing upon them, and likewise for grazing and agricultural purposes.

"It is also in evidence that this reservation was occupied. in accordance with the executive order, until the year 1861, when a great freshet occurred, which washed away all the houses and improvements which had been erected thereon. Early in the following year (1862) the Indians were removed by official direction temporarily to Smith's

River, and soon thereafter to the Hoopa Reservation on Trinity River, where they were permanently located, and an agency established for their benefit.

"After this destruction of the Indian settlements and public property by the freshet of 1861, which was undoubtedly the primary cause of the removal of the Indians from the Klamath River Reservation to that of the Hoopa Valley on the Trinity River, it was generally understood and believed that the Government had abandoned all claim to the lands embraced within this reservation. As a result of such belief and understanding, citizens of the United States seeking homes in this portion of the State of California entered upon, occupied, and improved certain portions of these lands, many of whom expended large sums of money, and still greater values in labor, in the development and improvement of the lands in question, and the erection of their homes. To dispel any doubts that might have been entertained as to the rights of settlers on this abandoned reservation, in the year 1874 the Hon. J. K. Luttrell applied to the Department of the Interior for information as to whether the Klamath River Reservation was still held as such by the Government, and in response received the following letter, to wit:

DEPARTMENT OF THE INTERIOR,
OFFICE OF INDIAN AFFAIRS,
Washington, D. C., Feb. 27, 1874.

SIR:—In response to your verbal inquiry concerning the Klamath Indian Reservation in California, I will state that the reservation in question, being described as a strip of country commencing at the coast of the Pacific Ocean and extending one mile in width on each side of the Klamath River, and up the same twenty miles, was approved by the President on the 16th of November, 1855, as one of the two reservations for Indians in California authorized by a clause in the Indian appropriation act of March 3, 1855 (Stat. L., vol. 10, p. 699). In the year 1861 nearly all of the arable land was destroyed by a freshet, rendering the reservation almost worthless, in view of which a new reservation was established adjacent thereto by order of the Secretary of the Interior, dated May 3, 1862. This reservation was known as the Smith's River Reservation, and was discontinued by a clause in the Indian appropriation act approved July 27, 1868 (Stat. L., vol 15, p. 22). The Klamath Reservation has not been used for any public purposes since the freshet referred to, and the department has no claim upon it.

Very respectfully, your obedient servant,

EDWARD SHUTER,
Commissioner.

Hon. J. K. Luttrell,
House of Representatives.

"This official communication, proceeding from an authorized agent of the Government, was, of course, relied upon as an official declaration that the Government had relinquished and abandoned all claim to the lands of the said reservation which had been conferred upon it by the act of March 3, 1855. This official letter was confirmatory of what had been for years the understanding and belief of every one conversant with the facts in the case.

"After the publication of this official declaration on the part of the Government, through the agent authorized by law to give expression to such determination and decision on its part, settlers on the abandoned reservation rested in security. As natural to such an event, possessed with the idea that the title to their homes and the results of their labor would remain undisturbed, a fresh impetus was given to the improvement of farms, building of houses, establishment of fisheries, erection of mills, and many other processes of development incident to the settlement of a new country. In the progress of this development the wants of the settlers called for mail facilities, and a post-office was established at the mouth of the Klamath River. The establishment of this office was another recognition on the part of the agents of the Government of the permanency of the white settlers on this abandoned reservation.

As a further mark of the belief of these settlers that their homes and property would be reserved to them, they erected bridges and established ferries to promote intercourse between the settlements on both sides of the river.

"In the midst of this progress of white civilization on an abandoned reservation, in the year 1877, for some cause which is not apparent at this time, the Government chose to reassert its rights to this reservation. It appears that some Indians, probably those belonging to the Hoopa Reservation, had found their way back to the Klamath River, and were living, as Indians in that section of country do, on fish, supplemented with what they could beg from the whites, and when this source failed would perform such labor for the settlers as would procure the means of sustaining life.

"From the testimony of eminent citizens of the vicinity, who are well informed as to the facts of which they speak, and whose veracity is unquestioned, it is established that the whites and Indians were living in a state of peace, and also in a state of mutual dependency and communion with each other, so far as labor and food were concerned, inasmuch as the Indians depended more or less upon the whites for subsistence, and the whites in turn employed the Indians to perform such labor as they were capable of performing.

"It is in evidence that some time in the spring or early part of 1877 Lieut. James Halloran made a scout to the mouth of the Klamath River, and reported a condition of affairs likely to lead to hostilities between the whites and Indians if the cause of disagreement was not speedily removed. The inciting cause is not stated, but regarding the declaration of reliable and trustyworthy citizens as correct, that the whites and Indians were living in peace, and that the Indians did not desire the whites to leave, it is difficult to surmise what the "conflicting interests" were, or what the cause of dissatisfaction. There were neither agent nor superintendent at the Klamath River Reservation, and it is hinted that liquor was being sold to the Indians, but there were laws in force under which those who sold intoxicating liquors to these Indians could have been punished. There is no spirit of justice or equity in a rule that would make a whole community suffer for the misdeeds of a few of its members, and that punishment so great as to sweep from them their homes and property, the result of long years of industry, sobriety, and the expenditure of large sums of money in the development of the resources of the country.

"This report of Lieut. Halloran was, through the War Department, laid before the Secretary of the Interior, and, in turn, he called upon the Secretary of War to cause the settlers to be removed from the Klamath Reservation.

"Acting upon an order from the War Department, Gen. Irwin McDowell, on the 19th of October, 1877, ordered Captain Parker to notify the settlers on this reservation to leave immediately, and this order he executed by notifying fourteen persons to leave with their property, four of whom were admitted to be without the limits of the reservation.

"These settlers earnestly protested against being forced to leave at the time of year when the rainy season was upon them. Subsequently the order was modified, allowing them six months in which to abandon their homes. These settlers protested that they had lived there many years in the belief that they were on the public lands, and that such belief was strengthened by the universal impression that such was the fact, and that the Government had relinquished its claim, as evidenced by the letter above quoted of the Commissioner of Indian Affairs addressed to the Hon. J. K. Luttrell, Representative from California.

"Under this order, however, a portion of the settlers were removed or driven off, and at the time of their removal it is in evidence before the Committee that there were not to exceed 115 Indians occupying this reservation. Unimpeachable testimony of a sworn character has been submitted establishing this fact. M. G. Tucker, who has lived in that vicinity for many years, acting as an interpreter, states under oath that there are not to exceed 95 Indians in all now upon the reservation, to wit, 29 bucks, 50 squaws, and 16 children.

"Joseph Ewing, equally well informed, states that there may be 115 in all, to wit, 30 bucks, 70 squaws, and 15 children.

"Judge J. P. Haynes places the number at 125 in all.

"Both of the affiants, Tucker & Ewing, state that these Indians are of different tribes, families, or bands, and that they are continually at war with each other; that homicides and murder are of continual occurrence. The restraining influence of the white settlers, in the absence of United States troops and Government authority, is needed to preserve peace in the community.

"It has been shown that these Indians have made no advancement in the arts of civilized life, there being not more than five acres of land under cultivation by them in the entire reservation, and that amount is contained in small parcels around their huts.

"Should this Committee admit the power of the President to establish permanent reserves by executive order, there should be a protest entered against the manner in which that power was exercised in establishing the Klamath River Reservation. A reserve containing but forty square miles of territory, covering forty miles of water front, extending but one mile back from the river's banks, is, to say the least, preposterous. This reservation might just as well extend ten or twenty miles back from the water, on each side of the river, as one mile, inasmuch as no one can or will settle upon these lands outside of the reserve for its entire length, as they would be cut off entirely from the river, which is their only and natural highway. The injustice which has been arbitrarily inflicted upon the settlers of this vicinity is at once apparent. To permit a few Indians (less than 100 in number) to hold 40 sections of land, and thereby control over 400 sections, is an injustice, if not an outrage, that should not for a moment be tolerated. It is clearly established from the evidence submitted that from the year 1862 up to the year 1877 the reservation in question was abandoned by the Government, and that the Indians were, in 1862, removed to the Hoopa Valley Reservation, and permanently located there, where an agency was established and still exists. Hence it appears that these Indians on the Klamath River Reservation are not where they ought to be; that by and under the laws and regulations governing the settlement of Indian tribes on reservations especially set apart for them, they should now be on the reservation set apart for them, which is the Hoopa Reservation on the Trinity River, in the State of California, a reserve sufficiently large, as appears from the evidence, to accommodate ten times the number now upon it.

"It is clear that the Government exercised no control over the Klamath Reservation for a period of sixteen years; that settlers went upon the lands in good faith, believing the Government had abandoned the reserve; that in 1874 the Commissioner of Indian Affairs declared officially that "The Klamath Reservation has not been used for any public purpose since the freshet referred to, and the department has no claim upon it." These facts are to be considered in determining the relative rights of each race of settlers. While the Committee would not do an injustice to the Indian, they are at the same time unwilling to permit an outrage to be inflicted upon the white settlers who entered upon these lands in good faith, and under the sanction of the Government have made valuable improvements thereupon. These white settlers are, in the opinion of the Committee, as much entitled to the protection of the Government as other good citizens who by the power of the Government are protected from an invasion of their rights and the destruction of their homes and property. If it be held, however, that the Indians have an original title to these lands, and that the 100 of their race now living thereon would be wronged by the passage of this bill, it may be asserted in behalf of the measure that the relations now existing between these Indians and the white settlers are of such a reciprocal character as to warrant the conclusion that the removal of the white settlers would be an injury to the Indians remaining upon the reservation, as the Indians in return for their labor depend upon the whites for their food and clothing, and the evidence discloses that from long usage this character of food and raiment has become essential to their existence.

"There are other and conclusive arguments to be urged in favor of restoring these lands to the public domain. By the singular construction of this reservation, as shown in this report, a large area of the public lands, embracing many thousands of acres of fertile lands, are practically withheld from settlement and improvement. The Klamath River is 300 miles in length, taking its source near the Oregon line. The stream is now navigable for 40 miles, and by a slight expense in the removal of rocks from the river bed would be navigable for 100 miles or more. The climate and the nature of the soil both combine to render the commercial values of this stream of great importance. It is asserted by competent authority that this section has no equal in California as a fruit and wine growing country. Along the entire length of the Klamath River, and especially within the reserve in question, and back of it, are large bodies of the best timber in use, including redwood, yellow and white pine, and cedar. The natural highway to these immense values is the Klamath River, none of which can be appropriated to the uses and arts of civilization so long as the reservation remains as such, as private enterprise and capital is debarred from entering upon the developments and labor required to perfect their use. This river, whose length for twenty miles is locked by a despotic act on the part of the Government, is likewise the natural highway to an extensive mining country, which remains undeveloped and valueless for want of better communication. Private capital, always cautious, will not seek investment, no matter what results may be offered, in sections of the country where settlers have been driven from their homes by the strong arm of the military.

"It is the opinion of the Committee, after careful investigation, that the Government can have no use for these lands as an Indian reservation. The Hoopa Reservation, to which the Indians were removed and settled upon after the freshet in 1862, is located but 15 miles from the abandoned Klamath Reservation, and is capable of sustaining many thousands more of Indians than are now located upon it. Why, then, should these lands in question be kept from settlement and improvement by white citizens who are eager to expend their labor and means in the development of their resources?

"If there be no use for this abandoned reserve for the purposes originally intended, the Committee can see no valid reason why it should not be restored to the public domain, and again made free for the access of labor and capital of white settlers seeking homes and fields for their energy and enterprise. Entertaining this view, after an impartial and careful consideration of all the evidence submitted, they are constrained to report in favor of the measure, and they therefore return the bill to the House, with the recommendation that it pass."

It will be seen from the above that the Indian Department express themselves as being in favor of opening the reservation to settlement by the whites.

I have mentioned the great mineral wealth known to

exist in the reserve, also the vast amount of timber in the forests of the same. Before closing my remarks upon this subject, I will notice the facilities at the mouth of the Klamath River for catching and preparing salmon for market. During the fishing season the river literally swarms with fish, and with a large seine from five hundred to a thousand fine salmon can be caught at one haul. Not only one fishery, but a dozen large fisheries and canneries could be established at various points near the mouth of the river, and the revenue from this industry alone would be enormous.

CHAPTER X.

THE PRESENT CONDITION AND FUTURE PROSPECTS OF DEL NORTE—WHAT IT OFFERS TO CAPITALISTS.

The present condition of the county may be given in a brief space. And first, as to the value of the property in the county. From the Assessment Roll of Del Norte for 1880 the following facts in regard to land, improvements, stock, etc., are taken:

Value of land, $285,667; number of acres, 61,139; value of improvements on land, $13,512; town lots and blocks, $30,010; improvements on lots and blocks, $99,875; deduction on mortgages, $55,807; value of personal property, $308,240; money, $22,048; improvements on all property assessed to other than the owner of the land, $1,745; amount of deductions, $27,152; total value of all property, $899,738; value after all deductions, $804,144.

Value of script, $6,893; money, $27,373; 14 bee-hives, $39; 1,070 gallons liquor, $3,326; 525 gallons, $2,737; beef cattle, $75; 770 stock cattle, $7,961; colts, $2,040; 2,311 cows, $44,646; 126 utensils, $1,147; 137 goats, $402; 912 hogs, $2,258; 475 horses, $21,788; 135 mules, $4,875; 77 oxen. $2,570; 334 poultry, $808; 1,404 sheep, $2,675; total value, $128,827.

Taxes will compare favorably with those of other counties in the State, though they are higher than they should be. The levy of taxes for State purposes for the year

1880, was 64 cents on each and every one hundred dollars of taxable property, being an advance of one cent and a half on each and every one hundred dollars of taxable property, over that of the preceding year. Add to the State tax a levy for county purposes of $1.86, and we have a total taxation of $2.50 on each and every one hundred dollars of taxable property.

The trade of the county is small, and Crescent City, whose streets should be enlivened by long lines of freight teams and lumber cars, and alive with the excitement of mines and mining, is lifeless and dull. The principal exports are butter and lumber, of which 10,000,000 feet of lumber was shipped to San Francisco in 1880, and 322,000 pounds of butter. About $200,000 in gold-dust is also exported annually from the mines in the county. The imports are small, probably 3,000 tons of general merchandise per year.

Summing up the above, we find that the present condition of the county is anything but flattering. We find that the chief exports are at present lumber and butter, whereas chrome, iron, copper, and other ores should form the bulk of the exports from this county. We find that the value of the gold annually exported from the county is but about $200,000, whereas it should mount up into the millions.

Perhaps the reader will ask, "If the mineral wealth is so great, if there is so much gold, and copper, and iron, and chrome in the county, why is it not brought to the notice of capitalists who would invest their means in the development of the mines?" There is but one answer to this question. No one who has watched the course of the business men and other prominent men of Del Norte for the past few years, can doubt that the present depressed condition of the business interests and resources of the county is attributable to their own negligence and narrow-minded views of public measures and public improvements.

Other communities have embodied in their business precepts the one which holds that to be successful in trade a people must be enterprising; that without endeavor, nothing can be accomplished; and that if a community show an utter disregard of these prerequisites to success and prosperity, they will inevitably degenerate into a slow-moving, shiftless and unprogressive class.

There is no disputing the fact that the Del Norte of to-day is far different from the Del Norte of twenty years ago. Then, all measures looking to the development of the resources of the county, and all enterprises, whether of private individuals or of corporate bodies, having for their object the advancement of the material interests of the county, received the commendation and assistance of the community. No enterprise was allowed to languish through a lack of recognition by those whose interests it sought to subserve. True, money was plentiful and times were good in the early history of this county; trade was brisk, and merchants were making money and could afford to invest. But they did not rest contented with the trade they already enjoyed; they were constantly seeking new avenues of commerce, new markets for their wares.

At the present time, the fact is commented on by all strangers who visit Del Norte, that the community in general and the business men in particular are devoid of enterprise and energy. It has even been insinuated by some heartless critic that Crescent City looks like a deserted railroad town, and that when Gabriel toots his horn for the resurrection, he will pass it by---for as the inhabitants have never lived, it will be impossible to resurrect them.

Of course, the writer cannot fully endorse this extreme view of the case, but he cannot shut his eyes to the fact that the present condition of Del Norte is owing to the lethargy and carelessness of her people. And these same heartless and inquisitive critics have said that if a stranger attempts to inaugurate a new enterprise in Del Norte, no matter what they may lose by so doing the business men of the place will promptly and effectually "sit down on him."

The people of Crescent City have evidently read and profited (?) by the words of Horace Greeley, directing how to "lay out" a town. Greeley said that the most effectual manner to "lay out" a town is for the people to grab all the real property therein, and hold it at big figures----never sell it to a stranger for less than about ten prices. Never give a stranger any show. Put the screws to him strong, and----"keep him in the middle."

This direction of the great journalist has been religiously followed by at least a large portion of the people of Del Norte. If a stranger came into the county with the idea of establishing himself in business, he has been frowned upon as though he was considered a thief or a legitimate subject for highway robbery. In one instance, a new enterprise was projected on land in the immediate vicinity of Crescent City, and the projector was allowed to get fairly started in his preparations for work, and then his water front was appropriated by some public-spirited individuals; and if he said anything about being "hampered" or not given a fair show, the little story of what Jesus of Nazareth said unto Zachariah was probably related to him, and he was told "that's what's the matter." If he got a little angry and gave expression to his feelings, people laughed at him, and considered it a good joke. A stranger had no business to get mad----"keep him in the middle." And the appearance and condition of Crescent City shows that this course has been so steadily persisted in for years past, that it has most effectually "laid out" the town.

The present condition of Happy Camp is somewhat better than the rest of the county. A large amount of capital has been invested in mining property during the past few years, and almost the total gold product of the county comes from the Happy Camp mines. Hydraulic mining is yet in its infancy here, and the number of mines in the vicinity of Happy Camp using Hydraulic power increases every year. On the whole, that part of the county comprising the Happy Camp, Indian Creek and Bunker Hill mining districts is inhabited by an enterprising, industrious class, and may be said to be the most prosperous portion of the county.

The future condition of Del Norte rests entirely with her own people. It is in their power to perpetuate the present condition of things, and it is equally in their power to raise the county to a high standing among the mineral and lumber producing counties of the State. But to bring about such a result, the people of the county must show enterprise, liberality to all who seek to developc her resources, and, above all, the attention of capitalists must be directed to our boundless forests, as yet untouched by the hand of man; our inexhaustible mineral wealth, now sleeping securely in the hills, must be brought to the notice of miners who have the means and the will to work the mines extensively.

Notwithstanding the many untoward events which have retarded the progress of Del Norte, I believe that there is yet time to interest capital in the development of its mines, lumber interests and commerce. With this end in view, the following brief notice is taken of those interests in which money could be profitably invested.

First, we will consider the opportunities which the mines of this county offer for a profitable investment of capital. I believe that iron, copper and chrome will yet become the most important of the products of Del Norte, and as these minerals are all found in large quantities in close proximity to each other, they will be considered together. It has long since been conceded by practical miners that the only way to work any of the above minerals to advantage is to erect smelting furnaces at the mines, and instead of exporting the crude ore, to ship it in a refined state.

In the vicinity of the Low Divide, Nature has scattered her mineral wealth with a lavish hand. Every hill is a mine of treasure, awaiting the practical miner with his improved mining machinery and his indomitable energy and perseverance. Everything needful for the successful working of large furnaces may be found in the vicinity of the mines. Timber and fluxus abound, and no difficulty would be experienced in procuring all the water necessary for the purpose. The prices of transportation, coal, labor, etc. have been reviewed in a former chapter. The mines are now owned by men a majority of whom are unable to erect furnaces and extract the minerals. All the copper, chrome, and iron mines in the county, with the exception of the property owned by the Tyson Company, of Baltimore, could be purchased at a reasonable figure, and there is no better opportunity for the investment of a large amount of capital in the mining regions of the Pacific Coast.

The gold mines come next in importance as affording a subject for the investment of capital. The magic cry of "Gold! Gold!" was first heard in Del Norte on the banks of the Klamath River. From 1851 to 1860 the richest strikes were made in the vicinity of Happy Camp and on Indian Creek, and the cry of "Gold! Gold!" was echoed and re-echoed from the lofty peaks of the Siskiyous, until it rolled away and was lost in the recesses of the mountains.

But the "flush" days of mining in Del Norte have vanished with the years, and the halcyon days when the miner with his pick and shovel could delve into the hills and streams and bring forth the golden treasure, are gone forever. Almost without exception the placer mines of the county now being worked are owned by incorporated companies, and instead of laboriously working with the pick, shovel aud rocker, sluices and ditches have been constructed, and the powerful hydraulic tears at hills and mountains until they crumble down like dust.

There are large bars and flats on the Klamath River and on Smith's River which could be made to pay handsomely, if a sufficient amount of water was procured to work the gravel. Water could be found from five to ten miles from any of the flats and bars, but owing to the mountainous nature of the country, a large outlay of capital would be required to construct ditches and flumes to bring the water to the mines.

The gold-bearing quartz is just beginning to attract attention. Well-defined and extensive lodges are known to exist in various parts of the county, and the Myrtle Creek and Bald Hills districts are especially rich in gold and silver-bearing rock. There is no reason why the Bald Hills and Myrtle Creek mines should not eventually rival those of Washoe or Gold Hill.

Besides the minerals above mentioned, namely, copper, chrome, iron, gold and silver, it is thought that Point St. George is one vast bed of coal. All along the southern side of the Point, coal crops out on the face of the cliffs, and a test of the same has proven it to be of superior quality. Shafts could be sunk within two or three miles of Crescent City, therefore the cost of transportation would be small, and Crescent City could compete successfully with Coos Bay as a coal producing point.

The beach mines have before been noticed, and it is only necessary to add that they should receive the attention of miners and inventors. The man who succeeds in inventing a machine capable of separating the gold from the sand will be a public benefactor, and will secure to himself the wealth of a Rothschild.

The lumbering interests in Del Norte, as yet of little importance as compared with other lumbering points, is destined to grow to great dimensions, and the forests that now cover the foot-hills of the Coast Range will soon be felled by the woodsman's axe. The amount of available timber is enormous. It is estimated that calculating the amount of timber to the acre at 250,000 feet, the area of timber land in Del Norte county would represent a total of 59,675,000,000 feet. Calculating the number of working days in saw-mills at 300 per annum, and limiting their capacity to 25,000 feet per day, these forests would furnish material: To one saw-mill, for 8,525 years; to five saw-mills, for 1,705 years; to ten saw-mills, for 853 years; to twenty saw-mills, for 426 years.

The most eligible place for the erection of large saw-mills is near the mouth of Smith's River, on the sloughs which branch out from the river on either side, and form a net-work of safe harbors in which logs could be confined. The logs could be rafted down the river at the time of the winter freshets, and could be run up into the sloughs, where they would be perfectly safe, as there is very little current in the sloughs even during the highest freshets. The mouth of the river could be improved by an outlay of a few thousand dollars so that vessels could enter and load with lumber during any part of the year. Not one, but several large mills could be built here, all having ample facilities for securing logs and shipping lumber.

Another project, requiring a capital of $50,000, would repay a liberal interest on the investment. This project is, the building of the Crescent City and Waldo wagon road, from Crescent City to Waldo, Josephine county, Oregon. This road would secure to Crescent City the trade of a large section of country, and would be the means of building up industries heretofore unthought of in connection with this county. That the road would pay there can be no doubt. The present road from Crescent City to Waldo, built in 1857, is practically abandoned, for no work has been done upon it for years, and it is now almost impassible. The builders of the old road selected the least practicable route that could have been chosen, and the winter season generally left the road in a dilapidated condition, costing so much to repair that it was finally abandoned by the owners.

The new road can be built over a good route, passable nearly the whole year, and which would cost little for repairs.

During the last year the construction of this road has been much discussed, and many opinions on the subject have been made public, all favoring the belief that through the benefits it would confer upon them the people of all the counties interested would reap a rich harvest. It would be useless to give the various propositions for the construction of the road, for they have all, as far as I can learn, come to naught, and there is no immediate prospect of the road being built, unless some enterprising capitalist or capitalists come forward and take the matter in hand.

For the information of those who should feel an interest in the subject, below will be found the description of the route of the proposed new road, as surveyed by J. S. Howard:

"Commencing at a point on the old Crescent City wagon road, 7 and a quarter miles from Waldo, Josephine county, Oregon, at a post for the initial point, altitude 1820 feet above tide water, and run on an undulating grade (nearly level) to the south-west branch of the Illinois River, crossing the same at the present pack trail bridge, one mile and 23 chains from initial point, thence running up on a grade of one foot in 16 and one-half feet to the divide between the waters of Illinois Valley and Smith's River, reaching the same in five miles and 48 chains from station 0. The altitude of this pass is 3100 feet above tide water. Thence on a down grade of 1 foot in 16 and one-half feet to Shelley Creek at station 923, (stations 50 links apart, or 160 stations to the mile,) thence down near the right bank of said creek on an easy grade to station 1895, to a low pass about 100 feet above the creek which we pass through to near Patrick Creek; thence down on a grade of 1 foot in 16 and one-half feet or 3 and one half degrees, to the mouth of Shelley Creek at station 2492, or nearly 15 and one-half miles from station 0, thence crossing Shelley Creek by a bridge, span 50 feet; thence down the left bank of Patrick Creek, on an easy undulating grade to station 2731, crossing the same by a bridge of 70 feet span; thence on an up-grade of 3 and one-half deg. to station 2860, and intersects the winter trail one half a mile west of the Patrick Creek cabin; thence on a down grade from 1 deg. to 3 and one-half degrees to station 3280, or 20 and one-half miles to the right bank of the middle fork of Smith's River; thence down the right bank of the same, sometimes along the flat bottoms and other times along the base of the steep side-hills to station 3876, on the 24th mile; here cross the river by a bridge, the main span of which is 110 feet in length; thence along the left bank of Smith's River, mostly on the flats, to Gasquet's, near the 26 mile post; thence down the Gasquet flat to station 4366, where we begin to ascend the hill side on a grade of 3 and one half deg. Leaving the river for several miles to avoid the steep and rocky bluffs near the river, the route runs in the vicinity of the present pack trail to the south fork of Smith's River. At 29 miles we reach the summit of a low divide, and run thence on along the hill-sides on a grade from 0 deg. to 3 and one-half degs. to station 5240; thence down on a grade of 3 and one-half deg. to station 5409 to the South Fork of Smith's River, which is crossed by a bridge, main span of 105 feet about 60 feet above the water; thence along the left bank of the main river on side-hill grade to station 5750, where we leave Smith's River and ascend by an easy grade along the right bank of Mill Creek, through the heavy redwood flats, to station 5999, where we cross Mill Creek at the site of the present trail bridge, main span 86 feet; thence along the redwood flats to station 6336, where we start up the last hill on a grade of 3 and one half deg. At station 6493 we reach the summit, 500 feet above tide water; thence down on a grade of 3 and one half deg. to station 6690, at the foot of the hill on the prairie, about three miles from and east of Crescent City; thence to 42 miles and 26 chains, intersecting the old road 2 and one half miles from Crescent City.

"The road for nearly the whole length is below the line of heavy snows, and can be traveled at all seasons of the year. The formation is very good for a road bed, only a small portion of which is very rocky, and at all places material for a good top dressing can be had.

"In my estimates I have provided for planking 5 miles of redwood, which I think will be necessary to make the road passable in winter, There is no grade on the road heavier than 3 and one-half deg. or 1 foot in 16 and one-half, and only a portion as heavy as that. The route is well watered the whole length and there are flats at convenient intervals for camping.

"The amount of traffic may be estimated by the fact that the amount of freight annually imported into Jackson county, Oregon, alone is estimated by the best judges and by carefully gathered statistics at 2,000 tons, consisting of general merchandise, wagons, agricultural and mining machinery, salt, etc.

"Josephine county, Oregon, with about one-half the population, imports at least 500 tons; Happy Camp, in Del Norte county, about 350 tons; Fort Klamath and Lake county, Oregon, about 300 tons, making a total of 3150 tons yearly; most of which now comes from San Francisco to Portland, thence by rail 200 miles to Roseburg, thence by wagon 100 miles; making an out of the way trip of 600 miles, where it should reach in 117 miles via Crescent City. Now we estimate that at least 2,500 tons of this will pass over this road, which at a toll of $6 per ton would bring in $15,000 yearly, to which add tolls from stages and travel at $2,000 would give a yearly income of $17,000, which would be increased from year to year.

"The road when built in the manner specified will require but little attention after the first winter. The above estimates have been made for the import trade alone, but when this road shall have been opened the export trade in flour, bacon, wool and fine lumber will largely exceed the imports."

This road would be the means of building up a large trade for Crescent City, and it would be of great benefit to the whole county. Manufacturing industries would follow the completion of the road, and a host of new enterprises would spring into existence.

Another opportunity for the investment of capital here is, the building of a large woolen mill. Smith's River Valley would probably be the best place for the establishment of such an enterprise, as ample water power and a fine building site could be secured at a low figure. Indeed, it is likely that the people of the valley would contribute liberally toward the erection of buildings, and that they would also donate a building site. Plenty of wool could be procured. There are thousands of sheep on the hills of Curry county, Oregon, and if the wool growers could dispose of their wool at home they would gladly do so. The goods manufactured would find a ready sale, and the enterprise would undoubtedly prove a paying one.

A large cheese factory would also be a paying business. Some difficulty has heretofore been experienced because of the damp climate, but this could probably be overcome.

All of the opportunities for the investment of capital mentioned above are worthy of the consideration of all, and business men seeking a use for their brains and money can do no better than to turn in this direction.

What Del Norte needs, more than anything else, is capital—capital, the magic wand which will unlock the vaults in which our mineral wealth is sleeping. Capital is king; and his sceptre in waving over Del Norte will call into busy life a hundred bustling industries.

And when the lethargy which now envelopes our interests and retards our progress shall be a thing of the past; when all the forests shall resound to the hum and buzz of the saw-mill; when columns of smoke, rising from the Low Divide, shall proclaim the existence of smelting furnaces and reduction works; when hydraulics shall strip the hills of their surface, laying bare rich seams of precious gold; when town and county shall throw off the rust of idle years, and come forth into the bright, new existence of a better day; then can we look forward to hopeful prospects, and can truly say, "the night has passed, joy cometh with the morn."

The End.

DEL NORTE---OFFICERS FROM 1857 TO 1881.

LIST OF OFFICERS OF DEL NORTE COUNTY FROM 1857 TO 1881.

ASSEMBLYMEN.
- 1857 R. P. Hirst.
- 1858 John Daggett,
- 1860 W. M. Buell.
- 1861 S. P. Wright.
- 1863 R. P. Hirst.
- 1865 L. N. Hursh.
- 1867 T. H. Rector.
- 1869 Jas. E. Murphy.
- 1871 T. H. Rector,
- 1873 Jas. E. Murphy.
- 1875 Jas. E. Murphy.
- 1877 Jas. E. Murphy.
- 1879 L. F. Cooper.
- 1880 W. B. Mason

COUNTY JUDGE.
- 1857 F. E. Weston.
- 1859 E. Mason.
- 1863 E. Mason.
- 1867 E. Mason.
- 1871 W. A. Hamilton.
- 1875 W. A. Hamilton.

SUPERIOR JUDGE.
- 1879 Jas. E. Murphy.

DISTRICT ATTORNEY.
- 1857 John P. Haynes.
- 1859 S. P. Wright.
- 1861 S. P. Wright.
- 1863 R. E. Adams.
- 1865 R. E. Adams.
- 1867 Jas. E. Murphy.
- 1869 W. A. Hamilton.
- 1871 Jas. E. Murphy.
- 1873 Wm. Saville.
- 1875 E. Mason.
- 1877 E. Mason.
- 1879 E. Mason.

TREASURER.
- 1857 E. Y. Naylor.
- 1859 E. Y. Naylor.
- 1860 J. K. Johnson.
- 1861 J. K. Johnson.
- 1863 J. E. Warren.
- 1865 R. Dugan.
- 1867 Wm. Saville,

TREASURER.
- 1869 Wm. Saville.
- 1871 John H. Chaplin.
- 1873 John H. Chaplin.
- 1875 John H. Chaplin.
- 1877 Wm. Saville.
- 1879 Wm. Saville.

COUNTY CLERK.
- 1857 Benj. Reynolds.
- 1859 Benj. R ynolds.
- 1861 Benj. Reynolds.
- 1863 P. H. Peveler.
- 1865 P. H. Peveler.
- 1867 P. H. Peveler.
- 1869 P. H. Peveler.
- 1871 P. H. Peveler.
- 1873 P. H. Peveler.
- 1875 P. H. Peveler.
- 1877 P. H. Peveler.
- 1879 P. H. Peveler.

SHERIFF.
- 1857 N. Tack, Sr.
- 1859 Henry Orman, Jr.
- 1861 Henry Orman, Jr.
- 1863 Henry Orman, Jr.
- 1865 R. S. McLellan.
- 1867 J. L. Rigg.
- 1869 Anson Burr.
- 1871 Henry Doolittle.
- 1873 R. S. McLellan.
- 1875 Jos. Clark.
- 1877 Jos. Clark.
- 1879 Chas. E. Hughes.

ASSESSOR,
- 1857 Solon Hall.
- 1859 Solon Hall.
- 1861 Solon Hall.
- 1863 G. W. Russell.
- 1865 T. B. Thorp.
- 1867 J. Marhoffer.
- 1869 J Marhoffer.
- 1871 J. Marhoffer
- 1873 W. H. Woodbury.
- 1875 W. H. Woodbury.
- 1877 W. H. Woodbury.
- 1879 W. H. Woodbury.

The names of all other Officers have been omitted for want of space.

THE TRAVELER'S GUIDE.

SHOWING THE DISTANCES

FROM

CRESCENT CITY

To	MILES.
Klamath River, via Trinidad Trail	21
Gasquet's	18
Happy Camp, via Gasquet's and Waldo, Oregon,	82
Camp Lincoln	6
Fort Dick	8
Paecock's Ferry, on Smith's River,	8
Ford's Ferry, on Smith's River,	11
Kirkham's Ferry, on Smith's River,	13¼
Del Norte, Smith's River Valley, via Camp Lincoln,.	15
Del Norte, Smith's River Valley, via Tryon's Dairy,	14
Del Norte, Smith's River Valley, via Fort Dick,	15
Smith's River Cannery, (Mouth of Smith's River,) via Del Norte	17
Altaville, (in the vicinity of Copper, Chrome, Iron and other mines,) via Elk Valley	18
Altaville, via Del Norte,	22
San Francisco	280
Trinidad, by land	65
Eureka, by land,	90
Eureka, by water,	51
Rogue River, by land,	60
Rogue River, by water,	42
Port Orford, by water,	62
Cape Blanco, by water,	73
Coos Bay (Empire City,) by water,	111
Portland	300
Jacksonville	115

LEGAL DISTANCE FROM CRESCENT CITY, THE COUNTY SEAT OF DEL NORTE COUNTY,

To	MILES.
Sacramento	364
Napa	319
Stockton	372
San Quentin	292

www.ingramcontent.com/pod-product-compliance
Lightning Source LLC
Chambersburg PA
CBHW032156160426
43197CB00008B/947